D1073322

DIARY OF AN UNLIKELY WARRIOR

A Practical Guide for Spiritual Warfare

Angela Powers Flippen

WestBow Press books may be ordered through booksellers or by contacting:

WestBow Press
A Division of Thomas Nelson
1663 Liberty Drive
Bloomington, IN 47403
www.westbowpress.com
1-(866) 928-1240

ISBN: 978-1-4908-0116-2 (sc)
ISBN: 978-1-4908-0117-9 (hc)
ISBN: 978-1-4908-0115-5 (e)

Library of Congress Control Number: 2013912362

Printed in the United States of America.

WestBow Press rev. date: 7/18/2013

Table of Contents

In Memory of Shanda Arlene Padgett

I would like to thank Darryl Flippen, Vonna Burysek,
Emily and Corey Page, Robert and Betty Black,
Zac and Kristina Shannon, my daughter Brittnai for their hard work.
I dedicate this book to my grandson Elijah, and my son Ryan

Way of Life Ministries

"See, I have set thee over the nations and over the kingdoms, to root out, and pull down, and to destroy, and to throw down, to build, and to plant." Jeremiah 1:10

"And a highway shall be there, and a way, and it shall be called the way of holiness; the unclean shall not pass over it; but it shall be for those: the wayfaring men, though fools shall not err therein." Isaiah 35:8

"And from the days of John the Baptist until now the kingdom of heaven suffers violence, and the violent take it by force." Matthew 11:12

"And these signs shall follow them that believe; In my name shall they cast out devils; they shall speak with new tongues; they shall take up serpents; and if they drink any deadly thing, it shall not hurt them; they shall lay hands on the sick and they shall recover." Mark16: 17-18

"For in Him dwells all the fullness of the Godhead bodily. And ye are complete in Him, which is the head of all principality and power." Colossians 2:9-10

"And they that shall be of thee shall build the old waste places: thou shalt raise up the foundations of many generations; and thou shalt be called, the repairer of the breach, the restorer of paths to dwell in." Isaiah 58:12

Moreover the word of the Lord came unto me, saying, Jeremiah, what do you see? Then said the Lord, you have seen well: for I will hasten my word to perform it. Jeremiah 1:11-12

We were enjoying a good year and were riding high, experiencing a peace that passes all understanding. Our small group was going on our second year in ministry. We had started as a bible study group, just to study the word, pray, and fellowship. We had such love, respect, and unity in our midst that it was very refreshing. No one lifted himself or herself higher than anyone else. We had many years of combined ministry experience, and we were falling in love with the Lord more deeply than ever. We had done a task for the Lord, and felt pretty good about it. I know now, it was just a forerunner to what would happen next.

One of our sisters, whose calling is intercessory prayer, suggested that we start praying for our town, its leaders, and most especially the leaders in the Churches. We would pray for them to be blessed, anointed, and that revival would come forth in our town. We started doing this faithfully once a week. The Lord instructed us to bind the spirits of "apathy" in this town. So that is what we began to do. What has come from those prayers, no one could have predicted. The Lord's ways are higher than our ways. We just cannot understand Him fully.

I began having recurring dreams. We would be standing in the town square and the buildings would be glass, and would sparkle like they had just been washed and cleaned. In fact, the cleanness is what stood out to me the most, because by all accounts, this town is very oppressed and dirty. (Poverty was overwhelming here. People either have lots of money or none at all). Also people (in the dreams) were always old men, and they were loading their vehicles and packing up to leave. Old men in dreams are symbolic for old ways or old mindsets. I understood that these dreams were prophetic, because I certainly wasn't seeing anything like that happening at the time. We were also dreaming of battles and soldiers in military gear and guns coming after us. In these dreams they would search and search for us, but were never able to see us. The enemy would walk by us and look right at us, but not see us at all. It was if we were invisible to them at that time. "**He that dwelleth in the secret place of the Most High shall abide under the shadow of the Almighty; I will say of the Lord, He is my refuge and my fortress: My God, in whom shall I trust. Surely he will deliver thee with His feathers, and under His wings shalt thou trust: His truth shall be thy buckler and shield" Psalms 91.**

We were engaging the enemy in the heavenlies, and our prayers for revival were in actuality, militant warfare prayers. The Lord was only letting us feel and see the unclean things in us that we needed to change, and that too was a show of his love and mercy. Up until then we had been spiritually blind to many things about ourselves. He was delivering us one by one.

Not long after, I had another dream. My husband and I were standing behind a large piece of glass, when we saw tornadoes going up in the sky. (Tornadoes that start from the ground and go up symbolize deliverance). They would start from the ground and rise into the air. We held hands and walked out onto a wide porch when suddenly what looked like huge concrete statues with lightening around them, were falling to the ground. One by one they would land with a great 'BOOM" and when they struck the earth, the lightening would spread through the ground causing a great quaking. We stood and watched in total awe, three of them fell and I awoke. As soon as I sat up in the bed the scripture came to my mind. **"And He (Jesus) said unto them, I beheld Satan as lightening fall from heaven" Luke 10:18.** I prayed and puzzled over the dream for many days. I was visiting a dear friend one day and told her the dream. She said, "Oh my Lord, does that mean the end is near?" Out of my mouth the answer came forth "The Lord is showing me the wicked principalities in this town that are going to be cast down". Both of us got chill bumps and shouted "Glory to God!"

I have a Biblical dream interpretation book that I have used for years, written by a woman, the book is called In A Dream, In A Vision Of The Night. I pray that woman is blessed every day for writing that book; it has so ministered to me over the years! The large glass represented revelation. The porch can mean "outreach to the church; public place; exhibited; displayed; exposed." Of course I would learn within the year what the three huge statues would represent. I would learn more about them then I care to know. We would be engaging them in battle. A tiny obscure group of believers would be called to risk life and limb to overthrow them. We would be purged to the point we felt we couldn't endure it. The spirit of God was requiring us to cleanse ourselves, our flesh was writhing and bucking against Him, but our spirits were willing. During this time, we were allowed to "see and feel" how these unclean things had distorted, affected, and even used us. It felt like a battle that was un-winnable. It felt hopeless, but alas, the Mighty Lord would strengthen us. He put a warrior in us that I can't explain. Even one of our youngest members, who was fifteen years old, became zealous for the cause. She would fast with us, pray with us, and be one of the first to submit to God to get free. **"For the Lord God will help me; therefore shall I not be confounded: Therefore have I set my face like a flint, and I know I shall not be ashamed" Isaiah 50:7.** Our face was set like flint, and we would not be moved. We would think about giving up, but none of us could. So we decided to see it through.

Many years ago, I was in a Christian bookstore when the Holy Spirit whispered to me "One day you will have a book on these shelves". I believe that this is the book He was speaking of. I believe this work will find the right people, and will change whole towns and cities, I believe many warriors will rise up and take their cities back for God. Satan will dominate most of the world at the end times, but not the entire world. There will be pockets of resistance. There will be those who will cleanse themselves, and make themselves white, a spotless bride, waiting for our Savior with great anticipation. The prophet Daniel saw this ages ago. **"And some of them of understanding shall fall, to try them, and to purge, and to make them white, even to the time of the end: because it is yet for a time appointed". Daniel 11:35.**

I pray for those that read this in advance. I ask The Father to expand your vision and use you mightily for His kingdom. I pray protection and blessings over each of you today, in the might name of Jesus!

Chapter One: The Beginning

While doing a twenty-one day corporate fast, in the beginning of the third week, the Lord met me with huge revelation regarding the three principality Demons ruling over our county, and indeed, most of America, maybe even the world. In fact, everywhere you see a church; you must look for these spirits.

They are the spirits of Ahab, Jezebel, and Leviathan. It was as if I were awakened out of a deep slumber. My spiritual discernment was so keen, I felt unable to fit into the natural realm. Everywhere I looked, I saw bondage, delusion, and vexation. It was like a thick covering over everyone and everything!

"Woe to the rebellious children, that take counsel, but not of me; and that cover with a covering, but not of my spirit, that they may add sin to sin..." Isaiah: 30:1. I began to see that almost every male and female, in and out of the church, had been infected or affected by the three evil spirits and what I call their children (armor). I saw that these three spirits were Principalities that must be bound!

"But if I cast out devils by the Spirit of God, then the kingdom of God has come unto you. Or else how can one enter into a strongman's house, and spoil his goods, except he must first bind the strongman?

And then he will spoil his house. He that is not with me is against me; and he who gathers not with me scatters abroad. Wherefore, I say unto you, all manner of sin and blasphemy shall be forgiven unto men, but blasphemy against the Holy Ghost shall not be forgiven of men." Matthew 12:28. The context of this passage is about casting out demons. The blasphemy was about those who cast out demons. Because it is only by the power of God that these things cans be done. Having cast out thousands of demons out of Christians, including myself, I have little time for people who argue against this doctrine. It is a moot point to me and a waste of energy. If you do not want it, at least do not speak against it!

God began to show me the structure of the enemy's hierarchy, and I saw that it was God's people who were to blame for the wickedness and corruption in government, politics, and all forms of leadership. It is our sin that has corrupted the nation, not the other way around!

The Bible shows us that when Israel had an evil king, the whole nation became cursed. Judgment will begin with the church and their leaders. As I saw this, it felt unbearable to me. I felt the weight of my sin and all of my brethren's. I felt deep sorrow, knowing that it was us who have allowed the spiritual wickedness into our nation. **"For the time is come that judgment must begin at the house of God; and if it first begins with us, what shall the end of them that obey not the gospel of God?" 1 Peter 4:17.**

This concept was extremely difficult for me, and I had trouble explaining it to my flock. Are we to blame for the crooked cops, the corrupt judges, the pedophile teachers, and so on? YES! The answer is YES! We have blood on our hands. Our rebellion is the root cause of all manner of evil! I felt paralyzed with fear and trembled at the visions I was seeing, until God set me up and awakened the warrior inside of me. My husband, myself, our entire group began praying and repenting. We vowed to God that this was to be our cause. With every ounce of energy in our bodies we began to ask the Lord for a strategy, a battle plan.

God began to work with our group extensively through His Word, dreams and visions and just about every other way possible. We were told that we must root these unclean spirits from our midst, in our lives and our Church before we could embark on our next "mission".

I was meditating on these things when I caught a glimpse of Ahab. However, my mind would automatically go to Jezebel. He told me not to think on her at all until I had full revelation on Ahab. I began to see that Jezebel was a master at hiding her cohort, Ahab. She steals the spot light and doesn't mind being seen. What we failed to realize is that as long as Ahab is in place, she has power to stay. He is the more evil of the two. He represents the chosen people who give over their power to the enemy. Her witchcraft camouflages him so effectively; he is very difficult to see. I have dubbed him as the best "hider" I have ever dealt with.

She not only camouflages Ahab, but Leviathan as well. There is much written about her, and many sermons preached, websites full of knowledge of Jezebel spirits, but very few about Ahab and Leviathan. As I said, he is very good at hiding behind her. **"And the King (Ahab) of Israel said unto Jehosephat, I will disguise myself, and enter into battle" 1 Kings 22:30**

By studying how he behaved in the natural, we can see the physical attributes of the Ahab spirit. I had such a hard time focusing on him in the beginning, though I knew we must "kill" him first. Just as he was killed first in the scriptures. (1 Kings 22). Let me emphasize we mean to kill Ahab spiritually, because he has tormented and vexed and led into bondage the saints. This is not a physical battle, but a spiritual one. **"For the weapons of our warfare are not carnal, but mighty through God to the pulling down strongholds" 2 Corinthians 20:4.**

First Kings tells us much about Ahab. Omri was the father of Ahab who ruled Israel before him. **"But Omri wrought evil in the eyes of the Lord, and did worse that all that were before him. For**

he walked in the way of Jeroboam the son of Nebat, and in is sin wherewith he made Israel to sin, to provoke the Lord God of Israel to anger with their vanities." 1 Kings 16:25-26. The evil he did was that of idolatry. He continued to allow idols in the land of Israel. Ahab however is described, as even worse than his father, in fact, he was the most evil king of them all to that date. **"And Ahab the son of Omri did evil in the sight of the Lord above all that were before him. And it came to pass, as if it were a light thing for him to walk in the sins of Jeroboam the son of Nebat. He took to wife Jezebel the daughter of Ethbaal king of the Zidonians, and went and served Baal, and worshipped him" 1 Kings 16:30-31.**

Ahab was an anointed king of Israel, chosen to lead Gods people. He disobeyed God and married Jezebel, a Baal worshipper. I suspect Jezebel was beautiful and Ahab was a man of sexual lust. She also gave him political clout, which is also a sign of his lust for power. He threw aside the commandments of God for his carnal selfish desires. That is one of the fruits of Ahab, selfishness. He took God lightly according to the scripture; His own desires trumped the good of the people and the will of God. Ahab represents the chosen that cast aside their true inheritance for worldly, carnal things. That's another one of main fruits, carnality and worldliness. If they believe God's commandments, they don't think it applies to them, or their children. Their carnal lusts are what drive them. Ahab even permitted child sacrifices in Israel (1 Kings 16:25). Ahab refused responsibility, casting it upon his wife. In doing this he allowed his wife to be the spiritual leader of the nation. His disobedience caused all of Israel to stumble and be cursed.

*Note- Ahab spirits represents Godly authorities that have handed over their kingdoms (churches, homes) for worldly gain, power, and wealth. He represents the chosen people of God who get seduced away by the lusts of the flesh and the spirit works closely with the spirit of mammon. Love of money and possessions blind them to the true high call that is on their life. Mammon is a love of money, riches and material wealth.

In 1 Kings 21, Ahab sets his envy upon a good man's vineyard, and approaches him wanting to buy it. The man, Naboth, refuses him, saying that it was his inheritance from his forefathers and couldn't give it up. Ahab offered him a better vineyard, but Naboth refused. The Bible tells us that Ahab came home and lay upon his bed, turned his face away, and refused to eat. When Jezebel hears of this she confronts him **"Do you not govern the kingdom of Israel? Arise, and eat bread, and let thine heart be merry: I will give thee the vineyard of Naboth the Jezreelite" 1 Kings 21:7.**

Jezebel then hatches a plan, through deceit and slander, she has Naboth murdered. He was stoned to death, and Ahab arose and took possession of his vineyard. The rest of the chapter reveals how Ahab's pouting and passivity opened the door and allowed Jezebel and her witchcrafts to go forth through manipulation and slander to murder Naboth. However, God does vindicate Naboth in the end. Ahab men have many 'vineyards' in their life where they covet. Whether it is a new car, a new house, a new wife, a new this, a new that, nothing satiates the carnal desires of the spirit of Ahab. Ahab is selfish and rebellious to the bone. Many males have been infected by this spirit and are even born with it through generational sins of the forefathers, serving or being sympathetic towards Ahab. (Deut.5: 9)

The Bible doesn't really tell us much about how Ahab treated Jezebel. We know she was rejected by her father and given in marriage to Ahab for political purposes. My dealings and observations of him are this: He doesn't really love his wife; if he did he would protect and cover her with love, thus releasing her into her calling in life and to God. Scripture tells us that husbands are to love their wives like Christ loves the Church, even sacrificing His own life for it. Ahab men view their wives as objects, they may worship her looks, sexuality, or ability to make money, but they have little regard for her individuality. My instinct is that they are jealous of their wives. They dwell in mistrust, and selfishness drives their marriage. Ahab men can be passive aggressive, passive about things of importance, and aggressive about trivial matters.

Since Ahab is insecure, he must belittle her and bring her down, lest he feel small. His own insecurities drive him to double-mindedly worship his wife, while at the same time, loathing her. Many Ahab's had absent fathers and domineering mothers. This skews their view of women. On one hand they look to them to accomplish things for them and on the other hand they despise them for it.

Ahab in the Church:

In the Church, he looks like the elder or the pastor who is willing to look the other way. He never challenges blatant sin in leadership. He prefers his church to be more about having fun; he promotes the social club vibe, He always has a Jezebel and a Leviathan. He looks laid back and easy going, but he is the more evil of the three. He is carnal minded and many of his sermons are repetitive and basic. He teaches the milkiest of the milk. He may have a great personality outwardly, but inwardly, he is a hireling, not a shepherd, He will use his pulpit to bully people, but will never go to the person that has offended him in private. He rarely, if ever prays for his sheep. Any interest he has in them will be for appearance sake, or for financial gain. He despises the true prophets of God, only those that speak what he wants to hear. Ahab was a great warrior and conquered much land in his life. He was conspiring with King Jehosophat to conquer Ramothgilead, when the King of Judah insisted that they inquire of the prophets first, Jehosophat wanted to be sure what the will of The Lord was.

The Bible says Ahab gathered four hundred prophets together and all of them said "Go up, for the Lord shall deliver it into the hand of the king" 1 Kings 22:6. This did not feel right to Jehosophat, so he asked, "Is there another prophet we can inquire of?" Listen to Ahab's words. **"There is yet one man, Micaiah the son of Imlah, by whom we may inquire of the Lord: <u>But I hate him; for he doth not prophesy good concerning me, but evil.</u>" 1 Kings 22:8.** Ahab spirits do not want the will of God to go forth; they want to satisfy their own desires. As soon as you disagree with them, they will hate you.

In ministry every time we cast out the armor spirits of Ahab the person's face will contort and look like a pouting little boy. He wants us to pity him, but we must not! We must rebuke him in every way! Here are some of this evil spirit's characteristics:

* Avoids confrontation, let's wife, elder, or someone else do that for him. He doesn't want to truly be the leader so he flings it upon others.
* Compromises the Word of God (1 Kings 22:6)
* Believes in God, but doesn't want to be bothered with obeying Him. Their lusts for the flesh and the world are too great to give up.
* Can have excessive love for sports, hunting, and fishing. He prefers these hobbies to spending time with his family.
* Is not aggressive like his wife, men who have this spirit are often 'good ole boys' or 'laid back and easygoing' but it is deception. Ahab is evil to the core.
* Ahab pushes the woman into the limelight. She is the one who has a more abrasive or seductive personality. He likes to cast blame on her, but again, HE is more evil.

* Ahab cares very little for his children's spirituality. If he has children, he does not want to be burdened with them. He will either buy the child's 'love', or treat him with anger and jealousy. Ahab's assignment is to curse his own seed. (1 Kings 21:21)
* Ahab keeps ungodly order and subverted authority in place, causing rebellious children. Because he doesn't take headship of his home and kingdom seriously, he allows every manner of unclean spirits in the family. (1 Corinthians 11:3) I believe this is why we have so much gender confusion in our culture today; boys grow up seeing women lead and possess the power in the home, etc....
* Can be a workaholic or have gambling problems. He is the king of addictions.
* Can be very childish, sulking.
* When things don't go well he will blame someone else, he always has a scapegoat.
* Views parenting as playing with children and avoids the unpleasant things like discipline and structure.
* Doesn't care about his wife or her needs, tunes her out, and attempts to shut her up by giving in to her way.
* Does not want to lead, yet criticizes those who do.
* Financial curse, their covetousness will often outweigh their bank accounts. Many will have more than one bankruptcy, maxed out Credit cards, and very little to show for it.
* Condones and allows evil.
* Spiritual laziness (his form in the spirit realm looks like a snail. It has a hard shell on his back but is slimy, weak, and slow in body.)

Men, husbands, fathers, pastors, and elders must do their jobs! Be the high priests in your homes and your ministry. Lead your family and/or your flock with love and sincerity, and seek the Lord for them. Don't allow Satan to destroy your family, much less God's sheep (if you are a leader). It is your responsibility to tame your desire for fleshly pursuits, and be the head priest God has called you to be!

Do not manipulate, dominate, or lord your authority over your wife. She is your partner and God's daughter as well. She was meant to compliment you, not BE you. If you are domineering and controlling, you are a male Jezebel!

This spirit is genderless. Everyone has been controlled and everyone has been controlling. So women must check their hearts as well. Women who are leaders may also have this spirit. Single mothers are often ran over and controlled by their children. This subverted authority will ruin your child. The ability to discipline them is an act of love. Remind your children that you love them and speak to them about Jesus. Teach them morality.

Children who grow up without discipline are insecure, causing them to be controlling, and this sets them up for failure. They will vacillate between rebellion and rejection, as they are totally confused. Children are our inheritance; do not sell your inheritance for worldly, selfish things! See this through for your sake and theirs.

After casting out the armor spirits of Ahab (see chapter fourteen), we have found that it is a process of changing mindsets and breaking agreements with the Ahab mentality. Most that have this also have financial curses on them. This too may take time. Reversing the irresponsible nature of Ahab is indeed a process. But if you are sincere, the Lord will equip you and work closely with you in doing this. Now you can begin to identify the Leviathans and the Jezebels in your life. Remember Ahab's greatest sin was being sympathetic to Jezebel and allowing her to rule. You can have no sympathy for this evil spirit. Be prepared for it to use a wide degree of tools. If self-pity, crying, and begging do not work, it will try anger, rage, threats, or bullying. Sometimes they will even use flattery and gifts. I have never encountered a more cunning spirit in all my years of deliverance ministry.

Chapter Two: False Worship

As I said before, during this time, the spirit realm was clearer to me than the natural. I truly felt like an alien on planet earth. The next church service we had was a real eye opener to me on how these unclean spirits defile the sanctuary. As the praise and worship team began to play, the congregates began to lift their hands and sing unto God. However, for me, it sounded like fingernails on a chalkboard. The guitar sounded distorted, the drums were out of beat, and the singing was off tune. I fell on my face and asked the Lord, what is this? With my natural eyes I saw my church family, whom loved God with all their hearts and serve Him to the best of their abilities, worshipping in every way they could but it was distorted! The Lord spoke and said, "This is the nature of these demons. They defile the sanctuary and cause my people to worship me with false worship. He said, "I am allowing you to hear what I HEAR". I raised my head and I could see a flickering shadow moving around the room, landing on each person, moving around in a confusing, chaotic pattern. I wanted to flee.

When the worship was over, I was so relieved, though very disturbed. My people, God's people, were being hindered from getting into the true throne room. All our best efforts at true worship sounded like a high-pitched squeal, a horrendous sound in the spirit. **"When you come before me, who has required of you this trampling of my courts? Bring no more vain offerings: your incense (worship) is an abomination to me. New moon and Sabbath and the call of convocations- I cannot endure iniquity and solemn assembly. Your new moons and feasts my soul hates, they have become a burden to me; I am weary of bearing them." Isaiah 1:17.**

It seemed to me that our best offerings were so tainted that instead of blessing God, he was weary of them. **"When you spread out your hands, I will hide my eyes from you, even though you make many prayers, I will not listen, your hands are full of blood. Wash yourselves, make yourselves clean; remove the evil of your deeds from before my eyes; cease to do evil, learn to do good: seek justice, correct oppression: bring justice to the fatherless, plead the widows cause. Isaiah 1**

I saw God's sheep in a new light. They struggled to serve Him, the cords of sin had them so bound that deception was our reality. Here I was in a room with the most dedicated group I have ever been a part of or known, and our best efforts were as filthy rags. Our worship wasn't a sweet vapor, but a stench that stank to the heavens.

This made me so angry! I loathed these unclean spirits that had snared us, defiled us, and robbed us from the fullness of God! I felt a righteous anger, a desire to see them overthrown. Gone was all apathy for this false kingdom. Gone was all desire to tolerate these spirits!

He began to show me the snares and traps that had been placed in people's minds. Planted by the enemy, brought forth from the pulpit, and deposited into the people of God. He began to show me how the true Jesus, if He returned today, would be unrecognizable by His own people. We had made our Lord into something that he was and is NOT! Our programs and doctrinal boxes were so anti-Christ, I feared that none could be saved. In my despair His word came into my heart, **"The Lord knows how to deliver the godly out of temptations and**

to reserve the unjust unto the Day of Judgment to be punished... and HE delivered just Lot, vexed with the filthy conversations of the wicked". 2 Peter 2:7

I realize this is hard to swallow, and may sound offensive. It is difficult to me, even. But I feel that if we do not make drastic changes, we will have drastic consequences. I feel if we do not over throw this false kingdom, we will be overthrown instead. Anyone can see, even with the natural eye the moral decline and decay in our society, homes, and churches. Anyone can note that holiness is a foreign concept to most. Anyone can see that outwardly, even those who look holy have very little good fruit in their lives. Christians are plagued with disease, barrenness, poverty, and broken families.

Yes, my beloveds, Satan has been very busy, and since churches believe he cannot touch them, they have lost all knowledge of how to battle him, much less defeat him. He has been allowed to build the kingdom of Babylon through us. Those that do have spiritual gifts are trampled and overthrown. They are diminished and discouraged, persecuted and made 'little'. This is the fruit of Ahab, Jezebel, and Leviathan. Because people are not taught to fear God with a reverent fear, they believe that repentance is a onetime thing done when initially getting saved, they do not understand that humility is something that has to be achieved daily. Because of this mindset, we have become prey. **"For this people are robbed and spoiled; they are all of them snared in holes, and they are hid in prison houses; they are a prey, and non delivers; for a spoil, and none saith, restore. Who among you will give ear to this? Who will hearken and hear for a time to come?" Isaiah 42.** Who is he speaking of? Is it the sinner or the heathen? No, he is speaking of the CHOSEN, the ELECT!

One of my favorite things do when pleading with the Lord about the purpose and call that is on my life is this "Lord, I am but a girl, no one will listen to me!" He has said to me, in a firm tone, "I know your form daughter, I created you". You see this was a snare in my mind. A snare placed in me by many a preacher about my gender. I had to repent constantly for disobedience to God, while trying to obey man! (**In the spirit, there is neither Greek nor Jew, there is neither bond nor free, there is neither male nor female: for ye are all one in Christ Jesus" Galatians 3:28**).

I knew the many demons that I had discerned, faced, and cast out of people didn't see my gender when I commanded them to go in Jesus' name. But in the natural, I feared man; I stayed in a back room with the ministry God has given me. I flew under the radar, so to speak. This was man's plan for my life, not God's. Luckily I have a team of strong anointed people, male and female, whose strength and encouragement help me. They say to me "How can you do these things, accept God be with you?"

I say all of this to tell you that God has a plan for you as well, but so does Satan. He sees your gifts and can see into the spirit realm. You better believe he wants you to follow the counterfeit path and not the narrow way that leads to God. The enemy will tap into your insecurities and fears. He will use them to destroy you! If serving God truly and faithfully were easy, everyone would be doing it. Name one single prophet or disciple that had it made in the shade. I know of few, if any. We must expect opposition when we are battling for the Lord. We must expect to suffer. It is worth it! Your life or someone else's may be depending on your gift, your faithfulness, or your willingness to bow the knee.

Chapter Three: Occult spirits, Satanism, and the Red River Encounter

While I do not want to make this story about me, I can only draw on my experiences and revelation from God in my own life. About fifteen years ago, I was a born again believer, baptized, and spirit filled. I loved God and loved His word. Having been raised in a dysfunctional home, my experience with Jesus prior to my salvation was based upon my elderly paternal grandmother. She spoke of Jesus constantly, she always had her Bible lying on the kitchen table, but she was a woman of mental weakness. She was a shut in, an introvert, and was extremely fragile emotionally.

When the Holy Spirit began to woo me, I honestly thought that Jesus was just something old people believed in. The Lord began working on me at around age 21. I would be 24 years old before I answered His call. My husband's sister, who lived several states away from us at the time, would call us and tell us about her church and the things God was doing in her life. She was a member of a Church of God of Prophecy, and having battled infertility she called one night to tell us that a prophecy had come forth, that she would conceive and have a child. Miraculously, not long after, this came to pass.

For Christmas one year she sent a card that simply said "JESUS LOVES YOU". I placed it on a shelf by the television and every time I saw it, I would feel a strange yearning in my soul. Not long after that we went to visit her. Of course she quickly took us to church. I had been having female problems and the preacher that night asked anyone with illness or infirmities to come to the front. I felt as if a magnet were pulling me, I did not want to go forth, but I could not stop myself. My husband pushed me forward and I stood in line. Again, I had no knowledge of these things and I noticed he had a bottle of olive oil in his hand. When he came to me and touched my head with oil, I felt fire go through my body, and it was such a supernatural experience that it was hard to describe. I had been to the altar at Church as a child and had given my heart to Christ. I believe He honored my childish commitment to Him, and that night not only was I healed, but also I was baptized with fire (the Holy Spirit). **"I indeed baptize you with water and repentance: but he that cometh after me is mightier than I, whose shoes I am not worthy to bear: He shall baptize you with the Holy Ghost and with fire". Matthew 3:11.** Leaving the church that night, I noticed how everything looked different and felt different. I was truly changed, and I was now a daughter of the Most High!

It did not take long for Satan to begin to attack. Within a month or so I was in a horrible car accident, hit head on by a drunk driver, and what should have killed me left me bruised and banged up physically. Worse than that I had taken on a spirit of fear. Afterwards, I could not drive a car without having a panic attack. I was a new Christian but unbelievably, the Holy Spirit spoke to me the day of the accident. I remember saying goodbye to a loved one when suddenly a feeling and an inner voice spoke to me. I sensed danger, acutely but shrugged it off and went on my way. It was my first experience with the Lords voice. It was the beginning of when I began to listen for it.

I badly wanted to be baptized so I asked my Dad and his wife to take me to their church. However, every time I went to church, I began to notice a pattern. Every Church visit resulted in a severe panic attack. I realized that it manifested itself in the presence of God, and God allowed it so that I could see it, battle it and defeat it. Needless to say, it was through my sister in law once again that I would find God's mercy.

She had began calling us again and telling us of her new church, there were miracles happening again in their midst. During worship on several occasions, oil would seep from the walls. It was even covered by a local newspaper. Upon arriving, I was surprised to see a humble storefront building, and an even more humble pastor. (At this point all I had seen were cold, arrogant preachers, and I was starting to get fed up and confused about church all together). This man had an alter call, my husband grabbed my hand and took me up to the front, once again. While the praise team kept playing the pastor went from person to person praying for them. When he got to me, he asked me what I wanted from God, and I answered in a very rebellious way, "If you are of God, you tell me what I need." He did not get angry or discouraged but went and laid on the floor in deep prayer. We must have waited for hours and the musicians kept playing. When he finally got up he came to me and said "God has said that you have an unclean spirit of fear" and he began casting it out of me. It seemed to take awhile, but finally it released me and with it my anxieties as well. (He would later tell us that was the first time he had ever cast out a demon).

We went back home and started having prayer in our house with another family. A few weeks went by and this pastor called and said he needed to come see us. He and his wife drove three hours to our home; upon getting there he began to tell us that God had sent him to prophesy over us. He put us in a circle and prayed. He said things over each of us but to me he said, "you will be head of a deliverance ministry, you will walk in the gift of discernment", and he laid his hand upon me and prayed.

We were skeptical and stunned, but sure enough the gift of miracles and discernment in me that had lain dormant all my life came alive. Even in its infancy stage it was very strong and accurate. It provoked some jealousy and left me reeling with confusion. Here God had dumped this huge gift on me, a woman, and no one to ask what to do with it. I was terrified and excited at the same time.

Shortly after that the Holy Spirit put a book in my hands called The Pigs in the Parlor by Frank and Ida Mae Hammond. This book gave me hope and direction. Before long we were casting out devils left and right. The first demon I ever rebuked was out of myself. It was a spirit of self-importance. I was reading a book and sat up in bed and began commanding it to leave me. A foam-like substance came out of my mouth and I gagged it out. My husband rose up and said "stop that, don't ever do that again!" Of course I wouldn't stop, for it was my destiny.

Fast forward several years, my best friend and I was ministering and praying over a young woman who had come to us for help. She was terribly tormented and had a family history of Masons, Mormons, and Witches. That night I discerned and saw names that I had never heard of. I was used to the lesser spirits of fear, rebellion, rejection, etc.…but these were strange names. Puzzled, we dismissed the prayer service and later that night I decided to get on the Internet. When I googled the names, I was astonished that they were names of Deities and Goddesses. These names were names like Pandora, Arachne, and Artemis. I was reading away when I felt an evil presence. I turned and sitting behind me was a man, normal in size and even nice looking, he was watching me closely and suddenly I knew that it was Satan himself. I quickly shut the computer down and said, I WILL NEVER DO THAT AGAIN! I told my best friend and husband about it, and they were as astonished as I was.

I believe that that was the moment Satan knew that I could "SEE". I believe I have had a target on my back the size of Texas since that day. Afterwards, we began finding dead animals on our property, rats and chickens. We have a burn pile in our back yard, and they would lay them on the pile in a neat stack (no animal would do that), it appeared they were strangled. I know now that it was an attempt to get us to retreat in fear, and it actually worked for a time. But throughout my life, I have had such divine protection around my family and me. Financially, we have never struggled, Satan would put a disease on me and God would heal it quickly. Not one hair on my head has been harmed despite the multitude of curses that have been placed upon us. I tell you all this to warn you that when you engage the enemy, there will be opposition. It is crucial to walk closely with God, sanctify yourselves, and rest in his mercy and provision. He will never send you into a battle without equipping you with the anointing you need and the protection you must have to succeed.

Red River, the great awakening

In January 2002, our family was led by way of dreams to Russellville, KY. Our best friend had moved here and found a local church. We began making the one and half hour trip weekly to attend services, and soon were prompted by the Lord to move here. My flesh was totally against the move, but my husband was convinced that it was God's will. We settled in a home located between Russellville and Adairville, Kentucky.

Located about three miles from our home was a place known as The Red River meeting house. Apparently, in the year 1800, a mighty revival had broken out in this place. It is documented that people would drive in their wagons and set up camp on the property where a small log cabin church sat. The move of God was so mighty, that even skeptics upon arrival would fall to the ground in repentance and tears. Many would leave and carry the Spirit back with them to their hometowns and the revival spread, which is why the movement was, coined "The Great Awakening." I had always loved and been drawn to that place. The log cabin church had been replicated to look like the original building and it is now a historical site that attracts people from all over the world.

I had gone there many times alone and with various people over the years to pray, and every time would feel the Holy Spirit's presence. Our group, when weather permitted, began having services there. On several occasions, the anointing was so thick; you could literally see the "glory clouds". Several times we would receive a tongue and a prophecy, almost always, we would feel the Lord's presence in a sweet way that left us humbled and in awe. However, we would soon learn that the enemy also laid claim to that land. In an attempt to defile what God had done there, we would soon learn that Occultists and Satanists were drawn there as well.

April 2012

Our group of believers had been meeting in my husband's office for over a year. We had experienced the power of God move in our small group. I had taken to calling these brethren "Lovers of God". We felt unsure why He was in our midst so strong, but vowed that we would not take it for granted. We wept in His presence and marveled at His care for us. We were such a small number, about eight people at the time. We didn't understand why He would even bother with us!

Many times during prayer and worship, the power of God would get so thick that we would fall to the ground, unable to move under His mighty presence. It was one such night when I was praying with the group. Suddenly, the wall disappeared. Standing before me was a very large angel. He had sandy blonde hair and was dressed in a blue tunic with a gold belt and gold sandals. Then behind him, I suddenly saw myriads of angels, too numerous to count. I looked around at my brethren, many were on the floor, slain in the spirit, and I marveled at the vision. I wondered aloud, "why would so many angels be in our midst'? Very soon, it would make perfect sense.

Shortly after, I was awakened one night choking and suffocating. My husband woke too, because I was crying in my sleep. When I opened my eyes, I saw a black hooded figure sitting on my chest, with its hand over my mouth. I wrestled and struggled with it and found my voice, crying, "Leave me in the name of Jesus!" Poof! Just like that, it disappeared. My husband and I began to pray. There was an evil residue left in the room and we were frightened by it. I had faced and seen many a demon, but in my spirit I immediately understood that this had been a human being in my bedroom. I knew very little about the occult, even as an unbeliever, God had always kept me from such things. When many of my friends were calling psychics, playing with Ouija boards, and having séances, I had always been turned off by such things and stayed clear of them. (I believe this was the gift of discernment in use, even before I knew what it was.) Occultic things had always had such an unclean feeling to me. I never even liked horror flicks.

However, I had heard of astral projection, and soul traveling. The next day I researched it and found out enough information to confirm to me that this is what had occurred the night before. We called an emergency prayer meeting that night to seek God about this. My question was why? Why were these things allowed to come into my house?

That night the Holy Spirit spoke to me clearly "It is from the Red River, they picked up on your anointing at the Red River meeting house." I told the group, and they began making decisions. One person said we should order shofars. We did not know why, but we all agreed. (Shofars are the ram's horns that were blown in the Bible before battle, to call meetings and specific things). One of the ladies went online that night and ordered a set of four from Israel.

We were told it would take several weeks to get them, so we waited. Approximately a week later, the Thing visited me again, this time I struggled to wake up and I saw some dark hooded figure at the end of my bed watching us. I began shouting "I rebuke you Tanya, and I sever your silver cord!" My husband awoke and before it vanished, he caught a glimpse of it too. It was very eerie feeling. But somehow, I now knew its name. A few nights later I dreamed of an angel standing in my driveway, it spoke to me and said, "The identity of the coven that is tormenting you is of the Alexandrians". I awoke and went straight to the computer. Sure enough, there are two satanic or Wiccan movements, the Gardnerians and the Alexandrians. The Alexandrian's being the more evil of the two. The Gardnerians seemed to focus more on worshipping nature, but the Alexandrians were more satanic in practice.

The occult websites described how one must be very disciplined and devoted to be a "soul traveler". This was not something that your average witch could do. It is said to be very dangerous for them, sometimes having to do blood sacrifices to be able to achieve it. They described the process as lying on a pillow and going in deep meditation. Their souls could be projected by means of "The Silver Cord" (see Ecclesiastes 12:6). I had spoken "I sever your silver cord" the night it visited me, and one website said that if the silver cord is severed, or broken, the person would die. I thought, oh Lord, I may have killed someone! I do not know why I woke up praying that. I believe that is why it sat on my chest with its hands over my mouth. It was trying to keep me from praying. They discussed in their web forums that it was used as a means to spy, curse, and to steal energy from people. Witches and Satanists often practiced it on each other. Apparently to them, my anointing looked like powerful energy. However, coming into my home proved to be a mistake for them!

I found a scripture on the subject in Ezekiel Chapter 13. **"Thus saith the Lord God; Woe to the women that sew pillows to all armholes, and make kerchiefs upon the head of every stature to hunt souls! Will ye hunt the souls of my people, and ye will save the souls alive that come unto you? Behold, I am against your pillows wherewith ye there hunt the souls to make them fly, and I will tear them from your arms, and will let the souls go, even the souls that ye hunt to make them fly."**

Out of the mouth of babes

At the time I was watching my two-year-old grandson during the day. One afternoon while playing outside, I was sitting with my head in my hands. I felt so discouraged and downcast. My precious grandson was riding his battery-operated tractor. He stopped and came to me asking "Nana, what is wrong"? I answered, "Nana is not feeling good, sweetie." He laid his little hand on mine and looked up to the sky, raised his other hand and said "Jesus, come down and help my Nana. Amen." What happened next was truly a show of God's mercy. He went inside and came out with a child's horn that he had gotten for Christmas. He got back on his tractor and rode back and forth over our land blowing his trumpet. He must have done this for two hours straight. When his mother came to get him, she asked him to stop playing, she had a headache. I turned to her and said, "Let him be." She said he went home that night and did the same thing in her house too.

The next morning I opened my Bible to the passage, **"And if you go to war in your land against the enemy that oppresses you, then you shall blow an alarm with your trumpets; and ye shall be remembered before the Lord your God and ye shall be saved from your enemies." Numbers 10:9.**

After that day, no witch or entity ever came back into my home. Other members began to experience what we now call visitations, though. So we knew we had to obey the Lord and see this through. Now we knew why we had been prompted by God to order those shofars (horns), for he was going to require us to cleanse the land that Satan had defiled.

We had no prior experience in this, so we had to seek God constantly. Step by step, he gave us instructions. First, we were told to go to the land and remove and destroy and occultic symbols that may be there. **(But ye shall destroy their altars, break their images, and cut down their groves. Exodus 43:13)**

I was astounded the day we went to do this. I had been going there for many years and had missed the most obvious satanic symbols that were everywhere. The wooden pulpit had Pentagrams and multiple other symbols scratched deeply into the wood. I know now that Satanist assigns demons to these symbols as "watchers". They had been watching us all along. We took pictures, and moved to the outside. In the trees we found carvings, some ancient looking and some fresh of a symbol that at first looked like a J with a line atop it. We used a machete to cut out the carvings, and anointed the trees with oil. It took me several days to realize that it was a T with a curve at the bottom. I believe the T stood for Tanya. Whether she is the high priestess or the goddess they worship, I do not know. But the symbols were there. We noticed they were strategically placed on the trees in the shape of a pentagram, facing the entrance to the land. The perfect spot to "see" who was coming and going from the property. There was a small fire pit in the center. I believe this was one of their "groves"

We had moments where we felt very afraid and spooked out, but we knew we were being targeted and we could not walk away from this task. I now know that Satanist and witches actually get their strength from people's fear, they crave it because it gives them power. Once you stop fearing them, they have no hope of controlling you. Notice how occultic movies make you feel? Notice how satanic ritual murders and atrocities bring about terror? This is how their witchcraft becomes effective. Battling fear is paramount to winning against them!

Since it was a historical site, we felt we needed permission before we destroyed and replaced the pulpit. One of my team members contacted the overseer and explained what we wanted to do. He began to tell him that people had been calling him for years complaining of strange activities going on at Red River. For example, fires and howling late at night. He said he had given tours and walked in the church to find benches arranged in the shape of pentagrams. He said he just didn't know what to do about it. He gave us permission to replace the pulpit, and asked to meet with us. As of this writing, we still have not met him in person.

One of our team members is very skilled with wood, and the next week he built a new pulpit and we destroyed and burned the old one. The next thing God told us to do was to saturate the land with praise and worship and to repent for the wickedness that had been done there. We took our musical equipment the very next Sunday and did just that. The sweet Spirit of God was there with us so strong; I watched the faces of our group. They all seemed to be transfixed in awe of His glory. When the singing stopped, we fell on our faces and repented to God. We asked him to forgive those that had sinned against him, we asked Him to save them. I was so overcome with emotion that I sobbed. Our tears literally soaked the ground. I am not, and never have been a person that cries easily. This felt to me like the Spirit himself was crying through me. We went from being angry and afraid of these Satanists to literally begging God for their souls!

Others in the group had visions and dreams. One side of the property was an old cemetery, some of the headstones dated back to the 1700's. There is a stone structure that was the remains of a large tomb. Only the walls were left standing. In one of the dreams, one person saw animals being slain and blood trickling down the walls. Another dream revealed a group of dark hooded people doing rituals and dances around a fire that was placed in the center of the trees that I mentioned before. The depths of the spells and witchcraft that was and had been done there was sickening. We could not understand why anyone would do such things. How could anyone so blatantly oppose God? That is why I said before, our group was angry, and we felt no pity for them until God moved our hearts to pray for them. We took water and blessed and doused every area that they had defiled and broke curses off the land.

After this, the Lord told us to walk the perimeter of the land one time for seven weeks. We walked it in silence and met in the middle, one of our sister's read scripture, and then we would blow the trumpets. On the seventh week we were to walk it every day one time and on the last day seven times, and then blow our horns. About the third week in, God allowed me to see His angels. At the gate of the property, I saw the very same angel that had been with us that night in our prayer meeting.

I could see others posted at different places around the property, but not clearly. It was more like glimpses or flickers. These were dressed in the same manner and stood about sixteen feet tall. They were all male, and did not have wings. But the one at the gate was the most clear.

As I watched him, watching us, my group could feel a shift in the atmosphere, though they could not see him, they felt him. We were in the center of the land about to break up, but lingering in this peaceful, sweet feeling. None of us wanted to move. The angel began to walk towards us. I finally spoke up and told everyone what I was seeing. I was afraid to move, he had a huge smile on his face, almost like he was tickled at our behavior. I told him, "This guy is getting a kick out of us". I could see why, for we were very zealous for the Lord!

My best friend, who has served beside me for years, said, "Angie, go to him, he may want to speak to you." I stepped forward and went down on one knee. I was careful not to bow to him knowing that we are not worship them. Sure enough, he began to speak. Suddenly I saw the sword in his hand. He laid it atop my head and began to speak. (The top of my head had a sore spot on it for several days.) The words he spoke were sacred to me, but I will share this much. He said, "The Lord walks amongst you, this is a Holy Thing. He has anointed you to conquer with His sword." I gasped and fell forward. The others in the group began to feel chill bumps and the hair on their bodies stood up. They can describe what they saw and felt better than I. But we all knew something marvelous was happening.

The seventh week the Lord instructed us to sanctify ourselves for one week. We discussed what that meant, and finally just asked God to show us how to do that. We all look back at that time as the most peaceful experience in our lives. We had no strife in our homes, or anywhere for that matter. We prayed and rested in His mercy and waited for Sunday to come. We didn't know what to expect.

Upon arriving that day, there was a couple having photographs done for their engagement. We spoke to them and they assured us they wouldn't be long. We sat and waited for hours, as we feared the sun would go down and we would not be able to finish this task. Finally, we made the decision; we could not wait any longer. We started carrying the shofars (horns) and walking single file around the property. On our second to last lap, they were still showing no signs of leaving. We sat down on the ground and waited, trying not to feel frustrated, until FINALLY, they loaded up and left.

We walked the final lap, entered the center of the land and blew the shofars. We were expecting something big to happen so we stood and waited. One young man said he hoped he would see fire come from Heaven, or an earthquake. (You see why the angel was tickled at him.) But all we felt was a gentle breeze and a peaceful feeling. We started to leave and stopped at the gate to say a prayer of thankfulness to God. As we prayed, I felt a strange sensation in my hands; it felt like electrical currents flowing through them. So I reached over and touched the person next to me, and bam, he hit the ground. I went to the next person and lightly touched them and bam, again they fell. All of us but one hit the ground (he staggered and stumbled around, but never fell.) I fell last, and we lay there unable to move for a long time. It felt like His Spirit was upon us so strongly, we were unable to move or even speak. I thought, Lord, if anyone pulls up and sees us laying here they would think we are crazy!

Later, I researched the movement at Red River. There was a recurring theme of witnesses who had had the same experience. It is called being slain in the spirit. I had seen it many times in churches, but I always felt it was a little odd. Every time we have fallen, it was from a light touch or no touch at all. When I had seen it in churches, it always looked like they were pushing the person backwards; in fact it had happened to me that way before. This experience was totally different. We had no power to stand up, or even move, save one, and he even stumbled and locked his knees to stay upright. To this day we have not been back to Red River. There have been no revivals there yet. And alas, now I know why. Our work was not done, and God had only just begun. In fact, the task we have before us now makes that experience seem like pre-school training.

Chapter Four: The Vision Of the Enemy's Hierarchy

"For we wrestle not with flesh and blood, but against principalities, against powers, against rulers of darkness of this world, against spiritual wickedness in high places." Ephesians 6:12

When I began to see the vision of the rulers over our county, I bought a poster board and drew what I saw. I saw the principalities ruling just above the middle of the town. Attached to them were cords and the cords went down into seven churches. God showed me the three spirits and their characteristics.

AHAB: assignment- pursues world systems of power; promote selfishness. Bringer of curses to large amounts of people.
Keeps poverty in place because of rebellion and disobedience.

1. Cursed descendants
2. Condones evil
3. Hates Jehovah God's true prophets
4. Extreme Covetousness

5. Extreme financial curses
6. Condemned to death by God and seeks to condemn God's sons through inciting rebellion and irresponsible behavior
7. Works closely with strong man, spirit of mammon
8. Spiritual laziness
9. The best "hider" I have ever seen. He is almost camouflaged in the spirit realm
10. Doesn't like to make decisions / passes the buck
11. Causes spiritual stupor, blinds and confuses
12. Seeks to get leaders to miss God's timing, pushes and rushes things
13. Works closely with incubus/succubus, sexual sin perversion, lust pornography and addiction

LEVIATHAN: assignment – Oppose God through his people: stop revival and deliverance.

14. Blocks movement of the Holy Spirit through pride
15. Only the Lord can engage him and subdue him
16. False prophecy
17. False gifts
18. False praise
19. Counterfeit power
20. Controls by intimidation and strength
21. Rules many Pastors/Leaders
22. Keeps bondages in place through stubbornness
23. False humility
24. False vision
25. Mocks true authority figures
26. Works closely with Jezebel, allows her to have a measure of control and bring in her false gods

Jezebel: assignment- Murder God's true prophets/leaders. Sets up false kingdom.

27. Unholy covenants
28. Visible rebellion
29. Wants all eyes on her
30. Despises authority and seeks to injure, belittle or kill them
31. Haughty towards Godly rules and structure
32. Can be seductive and charming

33. Can be cruel, even to her own offspring
34. Uses eyes to flatter or curse. Jezebel, when manifested can always be seen in the eyes
35. Doesn't need camouflage because no one can make her leave because of Ahab
36. Has vision, but it is skewed. It may look like a prophetic gift but is done through clairvoyance. Will have some truth to it, but will miss the mark often enough to see that her discernment is false
37. Causes disunity and discord through either slander or flattery
38. Speaks demonic words (not prophetic) for people to swallow or eat from her table

Ashtoreth: Assignment- Engages God's people in battle, attacks viciously off the strength of jezebel's witchcrafts.

39. She is an underling of Jezebel
40. Aggressive spirit
41. Combative nature
42. Vicious, cruel
43. Two faced back stabber
44. Manifests as extreme anxiety
45. Works closely with Jezebel, if anyone dares engage her master, she attacks
46. Sends spirits of despair, lethargy, phantom pain and infirmities
47. Seeks to make God's people want to give up and hide

Chapter Five: The Vision of the Seven Churches

One of the things our small group did weekly was pray for the local churches. We considered ourselves a "pass through" ministry. Over the years we would minister in obscurity, praying for people and releasing them. We felt unequipped to be a 'regular' church. We had a very specific set of skills, and we were not afraid to use them. But just as it was in Jesus' day, only the ones whom sought deliverance ever really seemed to get it.

Have you ever noticed before our Lord cast out a spirit or healed someone, they were usually required to ask Him? We had wasted a lot of energy and time in the past trying to cast our pearls before swine. Most people were only interested in deliverance as long as it didn't require them to do much changing. Knowing this, we were very limited to who we could bring in our fold.

Over the years, Satan sent many plants, and our ministry was delayed three times. Of course, at the end of the day, it was almost always my own fault. God would give us warnings, and we would foolishly ignore Him, thinking we could still help. The end result was always the same, persecution, slander, and ultimate failure. I have always been afraid to speak against the church or any pastor/leader, because this is heresy and I had been a victim of the damage from it personally more times than I could count. So it was from this place, of total reverence to the church that God completely blind-sided me with this revelation.

I was in the spirit praying for the local churches, crying out for the innocent sheep when He appeared before me. He spoke and said, "Daughter, if you will calm your anger, I will show you". He immediately revealed to me this vision. In the vision I saw a huge mass that emanated energy and hanging from it were what looked like electrical wires, it was seated just above the center of town, above the park, and the largest church in town. The electrical wires, or cords, were running into seven churches. He spoke and said, "These are the seven churches that feed and strengthen Leviathan. I perceived the mass as being the principalities that ruled over our city. I was shocked to see some of the churches because by all accounts, they were the largest and most popular churches in town. I had even referred many people to them.

When I asked Him what the cords meant, it was revealed that these 'cords' are how spirits communicate and travel. The puppet master was using these to manipulate the people and infect them with unclean spirits. It is in fact this seat of power that we knew we had to over throw. As I said, it was not very far up, and my vision had not expanded to see who rules them, though I suspect it is Satan himself. I had been charting structures on the poster, like and architect, and God was showing me in visible ways that I could understand. I had seen these cords before in visions and in personal deliverance. When breaking soul ties and unholy covenants many times I would see the person attached with these cords. Unbenounced to me, occultists call them lay lines. **"The Lord is righteous: he hath cut asunder the cords of the wicked." Psalms 129.** See also Psalms 2:3, Psalms 140:5, and Proverbs 5:22, Isaiah 5:18, and Job 36:8.

I thought about the people whom I had referred to these churches. It took me several days to process or even speak of this to my leadership team. He said, "Do not fear, daughter, I have seven good churches, whose hearts are for me". There are 145 churches in this small town and it was unbelievable to me that only seven churches were truly for Him! I am fully aware that God does not need big numbers to accomplish His purposes, but still it was shocking and repulsive to me.

I said, "Lord, how can our small group come against these mighty churches, they will eat us alive! I have feared to speak against your church, don't ask us to do this!" He promptly replied, "You will not be speaking against my true Church, and every word you speak WILL be established." I immediately searched the scripture for confirmation (everything God asks of us will agree with His word) and found **"Thou shall decree a thing, and it shall be established unto thee: and the light shall shine upon thy ways" Job 22. "Know ye not that we shall judge angels? How much more things that pertain to this life" 1 Corinthians 6:3.**

Chapter Six: Stronghold for God

The Holy Spirit had been whispering to my spirit that we were going to be given a task; we were to build a stronghold for his kingdom. About nine months before our corporate fast, He began giving me recurring dreams. Many of them, we would be standing in the town square, all the buildings were sturdy glass structures, they looked clean and shined and appeared that they had been washed as drops of water were glistening off them. In every dream there were people moving out of town.

Usually the persons would look like old men, loading up and moving out. I know that this represented old mindsets. I knew the fact that they were leaving was a good thing. I knew that the shiny clean town made of glass represented transparency and cleanness of ways. Not long afterward, an opportunity came for my husband to purchase a building on the square for his business. Since our church group met in our office, it meant that we would be moving too.

It did not take long before we began to be exposed to the corruption and greed that was in power in our town. I had heard many stories of bribery and injustice, I was not from here and had mostly been obscure to the ways of things, but suddenly people started coming out of the woodwork, speaking of corruption. It was well known that if you had money or influence, you could get away with just about anything here. The stories people told seemed unbelievable to me. I know there are good leaders here too. But the 'old money' crowd seemed to be an empire that couldn't be moved. God had given me contacts with good people in political circles trying to make a difference. However, at the end of the day all were frustrated.

I sought the Lord about the word 'stronghold'. My experiences with the word were always associated with the enemy and his ways. I searched the scripture for confirmation and found it in Daniel chapter 11. Speaking of the anti-christ, it is prophesied that the son of perdition would have pockets of opposition. Though he would be given power to rule and dominate, not all would follow him. **"He shall enter peaceably even upon the fattest places of province; and he shall do that which his fathers have not done, nor his fathers fathers; he shall scatter among the prey, and spoil, and riches: yea, <u>and he shall forecast his devices against the stronghold, even for a time"</u> Daniel 11:24.** The root words for forecast and devices both mean, "to plot against".

I feel that there will be people all over the world, perhaps small pockets that will resist the Devil and his kingdom unto the very end. Our group seemed to be chosen to do spiritual warfare to make a way for this place to be used and strengthened for such a time. I also understood that we would have to tear down the false kingdom in order to do so. I knew it had to be done in the spirit realm first, and then the natural would fall into place. This thick blanket of delusion would have to be broken before God's people could hear him. I believe there will be places for people to seek refuge and safety. I am convinced that this place I live in will be such place.

Chapter Seven: Leviathan the Fierce

As God began giving us revelation on this principality, we realized that it would have to be dealt with before we could uproot Jezebel. Its strength was holding her in place. While the women were convicted about Jezebel, they weren't budging. This spirit was just unwilling to allow the persons to truly repent. I sensed and watched her go dormant. I had taken to praying and asking God to shield and protect us from Jezebel's witchcrafts as I taught and ministered on the subject of Leviathan. I have known from experience how important it is to stay in rhythm with the Holy Spirit. We can never get ahead of Him in battle. We had to start attacking Leviathan. Doing anything in our own timing and in our own mind is futile. As much as we wanted the witch gone, we had to go in the order God was leading us in.

I asked God to show me Leviathan and his ways and began to flood my memories with past experiences. Apparently, I had dealings with this spirit many times. The first example was the pastor of the first church we had attended when we moved here. This man never liked me. He ignored me and I could feel disdain for me almost every time he looked at me. Despite this treatment stayed on. I was taught that as a woman, I should sit quietly by and keep my mouth shut. If I did not, I was rebellious and out of order. I had never had a true pastor, so I did now know this was not okay. Soon some women began coming to me for prayer. My friend and her husband were having prayer meetings in their home, with the pastor's blessing. We began having deliverance sessions. The spirit of God would move in our home meetings, but several people remarked and noticed that if the pastor came, nothing would happen. It would feel very dry. I paid no attention to it. In my heart, I just wanted him to like me and approve of me.

One Wednesday night several ladies met me at the church door. A man in the church had been known to have violent seizures. They were getting worse, and we suspected it was a demon. That night he had a particularly bad one right before we arrived, and the ladies asked me to pray for him. No sooner than I agreed, I was met with extreme anger from the pastor. He sent his praise and worship leader to rebuke me, saying I was out of order and no woman could have any authority over a man in His church. This praise leader had been with me, his wife was gifted in deliverance and discernment too (She still ministers with me today), and he had seen the miracles that took place in our meetings, so I was very surprised at his cruel treatment of me. Later that night, he apologized to me saying that the pastor had commanded him to do it.

However, I went in to the sanctuary dejected, rejected, and sad. I fought back tears and was so embarrassed that I wanted to die. We kept attending his church. I felt I was to blame. I asked God why he gave me this gift. It felt like a curse! Soon it came to light that the churches finances were a mess. We were months behind on our rent, the water and light bills were always paid late, and we were about to get evicted. The core members of the church elected a finance team, and my husband sat on the board. That is when the pastor completely wigged out. He refused to give up any control of the church checking account or be accountable in any way. I had nothing to do with this, but Leviathan had been roused.

Not long after he was preaching on husband and wives submitting to one another so that our prayers wouldn't be hindered (that's all he seemed to talk about, wives submit to your husband's), when I said AMEN! At that point he stopped, and turned to me, pointed his finger at me and began to accuse me of being Jezebel. I was so embarrassed and hurt, I tried to sink into the seat. When I left, I spent many days crying. This wound was a deep one and just reaffirmed every other wound I had received from men, especially so-called pastors in my life.

One day I was praying for him, because I knew that Jesus commanded us to pray for those that hurt us. I knew I had to forgive him. Suddenly, I had a vision. I saw him in a pulpit speaking and moving his hands around, when a crocodile appeared and swallowed him whole. I remember its teeth were pointed and huge. I sat up astonished, and did not know what I was seeing. I now know that this man was and as far as I know, still is possessed with the spirit of Leviathan. A few weeks after the vision, a precious lady from our church called me to say how sorry she was for the way I was treated, and admitted he was openly still speaking against me from the pulpit.

My husband learned a lot from this experience. He noticed and commented on how badly the men in that church seemed to treat their wives. Speaking to them like they were children. Several women admitted that they even put their husband's shoes on and took them off their feet each night. He would remark to me, "I hope I don't look and sound that way!" It totally sickened him. God was giving him a perfect hatred for this doctrine. We despise this doctrine that keeps women in the dust, and wipes out some of God's most gifted daughters. We fully understand creative order and headship. But this demon was preached in just about every pulpit we had encountered up to that time.

All you have to do is look at some of the anointed women in ministry today, to know it is false. There were prophetesses in the Old Testament and the New Testament. There were female leaders in the Old Testament and deaconesses in the New. I believe it is an end time prophecy being fulfilled today. **"And in it shall come to pass afterward, that I will pour out my spirit upon ALL flesh; and your sons and your daughters shall prophesy…" Joel 2:28.**

I began to see a misogynistic twist to the Leviathan spirit. But in reality it wasn't my gender that Leviathan hates, it is my anointing. He is opposed to deliverance ministries most, and absolutely hates true people of God. Leviathan doesn't want there to be any movements of the Holy Spirit, he wants to **be** the Holy Spirit! Leviathan is the counterfeit to Him in every way. His characteristics are almost identical to Satan himself. The Lord revealed to Job the biggest revelation concerning Leviathan. **"Upon earth there is not his like, creature without fear. He sees everything that is high; he is king over all the sons of pride" Job 14:33-34.**

The second attempt our group had with Leviathan had left me so crushed, that I literally almost lost everything that mattered to me. I had severe bouts of depression, resulting in a complete nervous breakdown. My husband and I separated and almost divorced. I spent two weeks in a mental hospital. I did not even recognize myself. I had walked away from the call on my life, and this disobedience nearly killed me. Before I even knew what he was, I had taken on a huge spirit of fear of Leviathan.

Prior to this I had been enjoying a very close walk with God. I sat out of church for almost three years and worked on my relationship with the Lord. Many days I would spend hours with Him and the things He was speaking to me were too great to comprehend. The fullness of it, I believe is just now taking shape. I look back on that time as the most peaceful of my life. I was a wounded bird, and the savior was feeding me from his own hand.

I would go into visions often, and would find they were things being prophesied in the Bible. I horded these visions to myself and cherished this closeness with God. I was leading a double life. In everyone else's eyes I had a fulfilling career, I was a mother, and a wife. In God's eyes I was a seer and a seeker, my heart was entwined with His heart and I was madly in love with Him. I only spoke about the things God was speaking to me with my husband and my two brothers. I would share dreams with them and they would say, "Are you sure these aren't pizza dreams"? Both brothers would later return to the Lord and began having dreams themselves. They admitted that they all thought I was crazy back then. I was the most unlikely person in the world, it seemed, that God could or would possible want to use.

I put out many fleeces at the time, and the Lord answered them all. He began opening doors for ministry again. Nothing big, small groups here and there and I even traveled to small speaking engagements. The fruit started to come forth; some healings and deliverance were taking place. So the enemy laid another snare for us and we fell for it, again. We had heard through a friend about another ministry in town that was supposed to be about deliverance. We started hanging out with them. We felt the more gifted people, the better. But from the very beginning, everything about them was off.

Their meetings were always a "bash the local preachers" fest. And their fruit stunk. My husband repeatedly said to me that he got a check in his spirit about them. When I asked him what that meant, he did not know at the time. We were invited to a bonfire they were having, and I noticed that everyone was getting drunk. One of the leaders was standing around talking down about the church when I stupidly spoke up. I said, "That seems to be all you guys talk about, don't you think that is dangerous?" This did not sit well with them, and once again Leviathan was roused.

A few days later, the group scheduled to do a prayer walk. They broke us into groups, and as we walked one person would say they felt nauseous, or another would say there were getting a headache in front of a building, etc. It was very frustrating to me and confusing. I finally spoke up and asked, "What exactly are we doing?" They said, "We are discerning the spirits of this town." I walked on a little while more, and it all felt like nonsense. I turned to the two people walking beside of me and I said, "Let's ask the Lord whom they are. " I said, "Father what is the name of the ruler of this town?" Instantly he spoke to me "Baal of Peor". I told them and they looked shocked, even offended. A younger girl had Internet capability on her phone and googled it, Sure enough, it was in the Bible. (Numbers 25:3) The main leader, the Leviathan, looked at me and said, "You are a seer, aren't you?" I did not know what to say because I hadn't labeled myself one at the time. But it seems Leviathan knew who I was, even before I did.

The following Sunday I was to have my first service with them in attendance. We had about thirty people or so show up, and their group came too. As I went to the front to speak, I felt the most evil presence in the room, I could barely move. I pressed through it. Several of them were walking and pacing in the back, openly mocking me. I finally just dismissed the service and went home totally shaken.

The following day the 'Pastor' of the group called me and said he had been told by their leader to call and rebuke me. The leader was of course Leviathan, and called himself, "The Apostle." I was home alone that day and he began to rail at me and accuse me of the most outrageous things. He was out and out lying through his teeth. Nothing he said had any truth to it, whatsoever, and I told him so. He said his entire group was in agreement with what he was saying and had "witnessed" these things. When I told him to bring my accusers to my face, he was belligerent. At this point, I just hung up the phone, shaken and stunned. He began repeatedly calling me, leaving voicemail after voicemail.

In tears, I called my husband and asked him to call this man and tell him to leave me alone. When my husband contacted him, the guy insisted that we had to meet with him. My husband said that we would pray about it and finally agreed to a meeting with him, knowing he was not going to let up. We met with him and his wife at a neutral location. I believe he was functioning as the groups of Ashtoreth. His attack was so vicious and cruel, based on false statements and lies that I felt physically in danger.

When we sat down with them at a restaurant about two weeks later, his wife (who is very sweet) was friendly and all smiles. I sat there waiting and when he began to speak, I could hear no words, just confusion. I heard a high-pitched sound like a siren only with no fluctuation. I excused myself and ran for the restroom. I sat in a stall and put my hands over my ears. I said, "Father, what is this sound?" He spoke these words, "It is heresy that is why you cannot hear his words, they are heretics." We got out of that place and never looked back.

Recently, this person showed up on my Face book newsfeed. He is now claiming that Jesus is not the Messiah, in fact, David will be the Messiah. He wrote a long page about it and in my spirit this scripture came to me. **"But there will be false prophets also among the people, even as there shall be false teachers among you, who shall privily bring in damnable heresies, even denying the Lord that bought them, and bring upon themselves swift destruction." 2 Peter 2:1.** I did a root study of the word heresy. In Greek it means: sect or cliché, 1. Act of taking capture e.g. storming a city. 2. Choosing, choice. 3. A body of men following their own tenets (sect or party). 4. Dissensions arising from diversity of opinions and aims. In other words, they were clichés; they cause division, and cannot agree with anyone. They are troublemakers to put it mildly. In the words of my best friend, this is how far heresy can take you, even to the point of denying the Master!

Every time we had dealings with this spirit, it wooed us with flattery, showing that if need be it can be enticing and agreeable. It is a trap used every single time! Later, through dreams and testimonies of reliable, godly people, I knew I had been right. I now know the leader of this group, the so-called "Apostle", is a full-blown Leviathan. He currently has a position in a local church I had been a member of. I was the head of the women's ministry when he showed back up again in my life. I know who his Jezebel is, and who is Ahab is. In fact, God had repeatedly told me to look at them as the physical embodiment of how these spirits rule. When I walked in the church that night, and I saw him, I had a horrible panic attack. I had to go to the back of the church and pray! Not long after, God would remove us from that church. His Jezebel began slandering me to the pastor and to the women (she has great power there because of her wealth). Soon the pastor had a falling out with my husband, who served as an elder. We left quietly. We did not try and take folks with us or cause problems. I believe it was God's will because of the very mission we are on now.

Prior to Leviathan coming, I had been hearing the Lord for that church. I had dreams and visions. I would go to the pastor and warn him, but he shrugged me off. I stopped having words for them, and I asked the Lord why. He said to me, "You will have no more visions for them, and they will not see me again until they say, blessed is he who comes in the name of the Lord". I thank God that this time it did not hinder us, and there is no bitterness on our part towards them. We still pray for them and we believe God for them to this day. Our team would do warfare for them, and pray for them in a heartbeat if asked.

There would be a third Leviathan spirit come into our life, just as the ministry we have now was being birthed. I will give detail of him later. This one did little damage, because he had no Ahab or Jezebel to lift him up in our midst. He did no major damage, save delaying things for a few months. God spared us quickly from him.

People who have the Leviathan spirit truly believe they are the mouthpieces of God. Since no one else hears God like them, they do not have to submit to anyone else. They brag about their anointing to anyone and everyone that will listen. You have to look closely at their fruit to see the deception. They mock privately and openly, anyone who has a ministry or anointing. They cannot stand even the slightest movement of God, unless it is a false move. They speak with 'great swelling words' and allure the most vulnerable sheep. The Bible says they have a worldly life. Many will drink and curse. Critical spirits and accusations are common in them. They will be haughty and speak haughty things. **"But these speak evil of these things which they know not; but what they know naturally, as brute beasts, in those things they corrupt themselves." Jude 1:10**

They will say things like "bring it on devil" and "I dare you, Satan, you don't know who you are messing with." What may look like confidence is really pride, excessive pride. Anyone truly called to deliverance ministry, casting out demons, and spiritual warfare, understands that you have to remain humble unto God. It is HIS power that expels demons and works miracles. (Luke 11:20) If we are his vessel, we shouldn't boast in it. The Lord is God, and He shares HIS glory with no one! And we should not expect Him to. You must walk humbly before your people. Transparency to your leadership team is key. You must be approachable. There are safeguards in the scripture to protect wolves from devouring you (1 Timothy 5:1). You must be willing to lay down your life for the true sheep and you must protect them from the wolves (see John chapter 10). They are in need of many things, we should be willing to pray and war for them, as long as they are willing to war themselves. You cannot behave like a 'hireling' and defeat the enemy.

Leviathans have problems with an untamed tongue. They use it to curse, belittle, and revile. They walk in mockery and will laugh out loud in church, inappropriately. They tend to backbite, slander, and gossip. Tale bearing is a common fruit in them. Let's look deeper at Job Chapter 41.

"Can you draw out Leviathan with a fish hook? Or press down his tongue with a cord?" Job 41:1. This speaks of his untamed tongue. You in your human strength cannot stop Leviathan and his cursing, boasting tongue. He can do great damage with it. But at the Day of Judgment we will all have to give account for every 'idle' word we speak. **"Can you put a rope into his nose? Or pierce his jaw with a hook?' Job 41:2.** This describes his UN submissive behavior. Leviathan will become very agitated if you try to speak to them, or reason with them. If you disagree with him in any way, expect wrath!

"Will he make many supplications to you (begging to be spared), will he speak soft words to you to coax you to spare him?" Job 41:3. No, he will not. He will not apologize or relent. He will attack you with anger, extreme anger! He feels he is above you anyway. You are not worth his time. **"Will he make a covenant with you to take him for your servant forever?" Job 41:4.** The only covenant he desires to make with you are to be on HIS terms. He has no intention of serving God's people. They are to serve HIM.

"Lay your hand upon it! Remember your battle with him; you will not do so again." Job 41:8. This is a warning to stay clear of the Leviathans that refuse deliverance. You may recall how my husband, our ministry, and myself was damaged, broken, and temporarily destroyed by this spirit. If you do not know what you are dealing with, his demonic strength will overtake you. It is vital to recognize who he really is. It is vital to make sure you have been delivered of all spirits of pride yourself, before engaging him. It is most vital to walk closely with the Lord. Remember, I had taken on an unholy spirit of fear of him, to the point that I feared him above God. I paid dearly for this mistake.

"Behold, the hope of (his assailant) is disappointed; cast down even at the sight of him" Job 41:8. Fear and trembling would grip me every time I had a chance encounter with the man. And I will also note that I was severely depressed, and even spent two weeks in a mental hospital. I was so depressed (and I didn't know why) that I even attempted suicide! The hand of God was the only thing that saved me from literal death!

"No one is so fierce that dares to stir up (the crocodile); who then is he that can stand before me (the beast's creator)?" Job 41:10. At the time of this writing I have been binding many Leviathan spirits and asking God to dry up his waters, to put a hook in his mouth, and to press his tongue down with a cord. After our group prayed this together in unity, that night as I went to bed, I would close my eyes and see a reddish colored dragon flopping like a fish out of water. I told my husband and friend that it seemed like it couldn't get any oxygen. My friend remarked, "We have been asking God to dry up his waters." This verse clearly shows us that, though he may be mighty and fierce, even he cannot stand before Mighty God. Jesus defeated him at the cross and through his sacrifice, so can we.

I was a bit puzzled to see the appearance of a dragon. Up to that point I had only seen his form as a crocodile. I searched the scripture and found this, **"In that day the Lord with his score and great and strong sword shall punish Leviathan the piercing serpent, even Leviathan that crooked serpent; and he shall slay the dragon that is in the sea" Isaiah 27:1.** I began to understand that when I had seen the crocodile, it was when praying over people; it was the lesser pride spirits of Leviathan. The dragon was the actual form of the Leviathan in the heavenlies, their master. Our prayers were affecting the big boy, the top dog in this town.

"His scales are his pride, shut up together as with a close seal. One is so near to another that no air can come between them" Job 41:15-16. Leviathan's armor of pride closes around him so tightly that not even the Holy Spirit can penetrate it. Air is symbolic for the Holy Spirit. We know that God opposes the proud, and actually resists them. So therefore, his ways are in total opposition to the Most High God!

In this way, Leviathan snuffs out the movement of the Holy Spirit. He snuffs out the prophetic and Rhema word of God. He squishes the anointing right out of you and me, if we allow him to. Whatever he teaches is false, he is the counterfeit, and to vulnerable Christians it may look like he is anointed. It is my practice to bind him, and bind the false before I pray and before we have services. When doing that, those that are subject to him, stand there confused, unable to worship at all.

Those who got deliverance from him state that they have to learn how to pray and worship all over again. They were so bound by the false, that the true move of the Holy Spirit feels awkward to them. Leviathan likes to incite emotionalism during worship, if he can't do that, he will bring in dead, dry worship. **"They are joined one to another; they stick together so that they cannot be separated". Job 41:17.** I believe these are lesser demons put in place as his armor. Spirits such as haughtiness, stubborness, and mockery, etc. They join together during deliverance sessions to resist the deliverance minister and the Lord. Praying for them feels like you are praying for a cold, hard stone.

"His sneezing's flash forth like light; and his eyes are like the eyelids of the morning, out of his nostrils goes forth smoke, as out of a seething pot over a fire rushes" Job 41:18-19. Some believe that this represents false praise and prayers coming from the mouth of Leviathan. Since smoke is indicative of prayers in symbolism, I agree with this revelation. His eyelids being like 'dawn' indicates how he can look very much like the Lord. The root word for eyelids is 'Aph'. Aph in Hebrew means 'of dawn, rays of sun'. The root word for morning is "Schachar", in Hebrew meaning "light, morning, whence riseth". God is showing us that he can look like an angel of light and he can mimic holiness.

I also want to expound on this through a dream that I describe in more detail later. I was awakened and sat up in my bed (in the dream) and I knew an intruder was in my house. I grabbed a phone and dialed 911 and exclaimed "Help!' The man on the phone said, "Are sure it is a fire?" I was looking out the window and saw a line of fire in the backyard. When I looked again I saw it was just a line of smoke. A woman's voice came over the line and said, "I knew he would be coming there." At that point in the dream, I lit a candle and it illuminated the whole house, sure enough there was a Leviathan in the house. In dream symbolism calling 911 can mean calling God or someone in authority. It was interesting that I never said to the man what I need help for.I pondered this for many days and realized that the smoke and the fire were just an illusion. I was focusing on it while knowing all the while that an intruder was inside my home. So to me, the smoke and fire (false praise and prayers) are an illusion and a covering that keeps us from seeing who he really is, a beast. The seething pot in the scripture represents the turmoil and confusion of those who sit under him.

"His breath kindles coals, and flames go forth from his mouth" Job 41:20. This is indicative of Leviathan's ability to spread discord. He intends to destroy the works of the Holy Spirit, and will speak against anyone who opposes him or threatens his status. He is unmerciful, and has no compassion for God's sheep. If they cross him, they will be persecuted and reviled.

"In the crocodile's neck abides his strength, and terror dances before him" Job 41:31. The Bible speaks of those who oppose God as stiff-necked people. They are very stubborn, unyielding, and unrepentant. There stubbornness gives them strength, causing God to smite them. Man cannot move or defeat them, only our Lord. Leviathan uses intimidation and will say that those who oppose him may die or be cursed with a curse. He bullies people into submission. Many cult leaders use this tactic to control the people with, Intimidation and terror. They say things like, "If you leave, you will go to hell…etc.".

"He makes the deep boil like a pot; he makes the sea like a pot of ointment" Job 41:31. The sea in scripture is symbolic for 'many peoples.' I take this to mean that in people's confusion and fear of him, that they will actually soothe him with ointment. They give him his power, they fear him above God. The deep is referring to the inner most part of man. That is the place where the Holy Spirit resides. It is the place God speaks to us. The scripture states that 'deep calls unto deep'. It is impossible to go deeper with the Lord when Leviathan is present. As I said before, he desires to be the Holy Spirit. He is the counterfeit. He resides and commands the parts of man that God desires to rule. Where the Lord brings peace, Leviathan brings a boiling.

"He beholds all high things; he is King over all the children of pride." Job 41:34. He looks upon mankind, and sees them in their pride, and then he becomes their king. I believe all have been tainted with some form of pride. I believe all require deliverance from him.

Do I believe that all are possessed with deities? No, I do not, but if you carry his children (armor), then he can pull your strings. When casting out lesser demons, they will summon these principalities to give them strength in resisting deliverance. I do know some that are fully possessed with these spirits, and sadly most of them stand in pulpits, or other forms of church leadership. This may sound harsh, but remember, I am a pastor myself. Satan has assigned many demons to my husband and me over the years. We have had to have multiple deliverances. We leaders have much more influence, and people look to us for counsel and wisdom, so it makes perfect sense that our enemy would target us most.

When dealing with spirits of pride, the person will usually have neck pain (stiff neck). They may have spinal tenderness because these spirits coil around the spine. Some feel a squeezing sensation in their chest. I have seen more than one person writhe like a serpent, twisting their head back and forth. Through the blood and authority of Jesus, we have the power to overthrow and cast out unclean spirits (Mark16: 17-18).

I cannot say it enough; Leviathan's biggest assignment is to oppose deliverance, and the Holy Spirit. One member of our group felt led to repent and apologize to the Holy Spirit; she described how she had been having trouble praying. That was odd because intercessory was her biggest gift. If it had not been for her praying for me so faithfully over the years, I feel like I would probably be dead. She described how while repenting for ever coming against the Holy Spirit that something inside of her broke. She began to pray in the spirit and got deep into intercession. I believe when she did that we began to have more revelation and break-throughs.

If we are in pride God will allow him to oppose and squish us. **"For rebellion is the sin of witchcraft, and stubbornness is as iniquity and idolatry. Because thou have rejected the word of the Lord, he hath also rejected thee from being King." 1 Samuel 15:23**

The prophet Isaiah states that during the end time, "God will punish and slay Leviathan for good." (Isaiah 27:1) Until that day we must resist him, rebuke him, and overthrow him in our own lives, our churches, and perhaps our cities. Jesus made the way and we should walk in the fullness of what he died to give us! His work on the cross gave us the victory. We must appropriate what he did. We must move the plank from our own eyes, to be able to help the brethren with the speck in their eye. We, as leaders must decrease and make way for the Lord to increase. Our self-will is a deadly thing when it isn't being lead by the Living God. Leaders who abuse and corrupt with their power will find on Judgment Day exactly who they are.

The apostle Paul speaks of continually pressing on for the prize of the high calling of God in Christ Jesus. He knew full well, that he could lose his own soul after saving thousands of others. He knew he would be pursuing Christ likeness until the day he died. At the end of Paul's life he writes. **"I have fought a good fight, I have finished my course,**

I have kept the faith; Henceforth there is laid up for me a crown of righteousness, which the Lord, the righteous judge, shall give me at that day; and not to me only, but all them also who love his appearing." 2 Timothy 4:7-8. Notice the words fight, course, and keeping faith. That was his life, and that should be our life too.

Pride, the Children of Leviathan

I have shared with you what pride looks like in ministry, now let's look at what pride looks like in a more practical way. Job 40:34 states that Leviathan is 'king" over all the children of pride. When we are in pride, we are serving the enemy of our souls and not the Most High God.

This is spiritual adultery, and is a bringer of destruction. It will cause you to fall, because you not only harm yourself, you injure and wound others. It will hinder your prayers to God and ruin your earthly inheritance. "**And I will break the pride of your power; and I will make your heaven as iron and your earth as brass; and your strength will be spent in vain. For your land will not yield her increase, neither shall your trees of the land yield their fruits." Leviticus 26:19-20.** This scripture clearly indicates that pride will affect and corrupt the whole land. It will affect your children and their children as well. It is a bringer of many curses, including poverty.

A very well known verse is found in Proverbs. **"Pride goeth before destruction and a haughty spirit before a fall". Proverbs 16:18.** Destruction is the fruit of pride. Broken relationships and problems getting along with people in general are common as well. If people say to you or about you that you intimidate them, this could be the problem. Many years ago the Lord spoke to my heart regarding someone who repeatedly verbally abused others and me. He said, "You never have the right to use your mouth to mistreat people, nothing justifies this in my eyes." **"In the mouth of the foolish is a rod of pride, but the lips of**

the wise shall preserve them" Proverbs 14:3. The Lord counts this as foolishness, and He cannot trust us with the riches of His wisdom, if we do not remove pride from our hearts.

I said before, the Leviathan spirits usually have trouble with their tongues. He berates, belittles, rails, and criticizes. Mercy is a foreign concept to those bound in pride. **"Blessed are the merciful; for they shall obtain mercy." Matthew 5:7.** Pride will keep you from even seeing that you have need of mercy!

People with pride are very hard to approach. They are very intimidating. People will walk on eggshells around them, and close themselves off from them. People with pride will often find themselves isolated, even from their own families. And because they refuse to bow the knee, so to speak, they are all to willing to sacrifice relationships to be "right". He is quick to rebuke others, but will receive no correction himself. He expects those around him to submit, but he himself feels no need to submit to anyone. Our Lord and Savior, Jesus Christ, came in the most humble form, as a baby and gave us the picture of perfect obedience and humility. He humbles himself at the beginning of the ministry by asking John the Baptist to baptize him. When John refused, Jesus said, **"Let it be so, for thus it becomes us to fulfill all righteousness." Matthew 3:15.** When Peter cut off the ear of the soldier who came to arrest Jesus, Jesus stated," **Do you not know that I can pray to my Father, and he would give me more than twelve legions of angels?' Matthew 26:53**

This is the difference between pride and knowing truth. He fully understood his power and authority, but did not lord it over the people. He had come to die for the sheep, and He was and is full of great mercy for us. However, when he returns again it will be with a sharp, two-edged sword coming from his mouth that will smite the nations. We must not mistake his mercy for weakness. Those that oppose God will be slain in that day (see Revelation chapter 19).

I have noticed a pattern with Leviathan; he will refute the true anointed in subtle ways. You can say something as simple as "Wow, the sky is blue today" and they will come back and say "No, it looks more green than blue to me." Watch for this fruit and you will see it. Leviathan is also called a "twisted and coiled serpent". I have seen this in action. When a revelation comes forth, they will somehow twist it and distort the truth, or claim they have revelation above it that is more important. If God gives them a dream to correct them or show them an area of sin, they will twist the dream and make it about someone or something else. It is always twisting the word of God.

Pride will keep you from seeking the face of God. In the days that we live in, it is crucial to be in a prostrated position of obedience and submission to the Lord. People who battle pride often complain of 'never hearing from God'. In fact, many say that God doesn't speak directly to man, and that, "that died with the apostles". When I hear folks say that, it saddens me deeply. If you are His true sheep, you WILL know his voice and follow Him. They will also stand on one revelation and build a whole doctrine around it. You can see these same people ten years later and they will still be talking about the same thing. The Bible tells us we will change from 'glory to glory'. We should always be growing, evolving, and maturing in our walk with God.

"The wicked through the pride of his countenance, will not seek after God: God is not in all his thoughts." Psalms10: 4. People in their pride believe that God already approves of what they say and do, so therefore there is no need to seek Him about their decisions. Others will stand on one revelation they received. Being puffed up about it, they never progress any further with the Lord. They repeat the same repetitive mantras, as if they are great revelation. And they are offended if others do not marvel at their wisdom. They basically are like a tape recorder, on repeat at all times.

Our last encounter with a Leviathan came about a year into our present ministry. He was well known in town, and seemed to be a man whom loved the Lord. We ran into him one day and he probed us about where we were going to church. We told him we are meeting in our office, and just casually invited him to come sometime. A couple of months later, he showed up at our Sunday night service. We were very pleased to see him and told him what we were about. He told us that he went to five other Bible studies and two churches. I thought that was odd, but was fine with it.

We began to notice our services becoming dry. We began to notice that every service he would sit on the back row and refute some little thing that myself, or whoever was teaching would say. He was older than us, so we respected him and gave him his room to speak. Every time he would stand up and repeat the same thing. He would say, "When Jesus died on the cross the veil was rent in two." We would say amen, brother. Then he began coming on our dedicated prayer night. During prayer, our group would play soft worship music and get alone with God. At the end we would join hands and pray together, each being lead by the Holy Spirit. He began to walk around the room and lay hands on people and pray loudly in tongues over them. My people began to complain about it. One man said that when he prayed for him it felt evil and caused him to have chest pains.

The next service the man asked, "I thought this was a deliverance ministry? I have seen no deliverance here." I went home and prayed about what he said; we hadn't had any real movements of God in quite awhile. One of our women was desperately seeking deliverance, but the anointing just wasn't there. The next service I had my back to the group, praying to the Lord and I heard him walking around (he always wore shoes that squeaked when he walked). I kept hearing squeak, squeak, squeak, so I turned and saw my group literally running from him. He would approach one and they would move away. Finally, he came up to me and for the first time laid hands on me and prayed in tongues loudly, I listened and waited for the Lord to speak. After we broke up, I approached him and asked him if I could pray for him. He agreed.

When I placed my hands on him all I felt was a stone cold heart. I felt stubbornness and pride in his neck and he began to twist his neck back and forth. After I stopped praying, he said, "What did you sense?" I said, "What was going through your mind while I was praying?" He answered, "I was thinking that it should be me praying for you." I said, "There you go, I sensed spiritual pride." The man then told me of a dream he had where a wolf was on his land, and I knew immediately that he was a wolf.

I found out later by chance that he has a reputation for being a part of at several church splits in our town. I went before the Lord and and repented to him and to my group for being a careless shepherd, I realized it was my own fault. He spoke to my husband and admitted that he really didn't agree with us and decided to stop coming.

Right after that, we began to get the revelation on Red River. God began to move again. I learned not to give my pulpit over to just anyone, nor to let people come in and try and take over. It is a fine line we have to walk, letting God use his children, but not yielding to the wrong spirits. I was guilty of complacency. I learned that when someone joins you, they should be in unity with the vision of the ministry, not opposed to it. Unity is most crucial in deliverance ministry. One bad apple can overturn the whole cart. When you are de-weeding a flowerbed, pulling out the weeds seems tedious and monotonous, but we do it because we have to. If we don't, the weeds will choke the flowers out. It will overtake the garden and kill the fruit. The same is with the kingdom of God. We have to pull out the weeds and tares from our flesh so that God can grow a bountiful garden that bears fruit and beauty. Leviathan is the weed that is choking out the fruit of the Holy Spirit in the church. He is very good at it. He has been doing it since the beginning of time.

The most startling thing about pride is that it directly opposes God, thereby causing God to oppose us. In fact, the Lord literally rejects us when we are in pride. He can do nothing with stubborn, stiff-necked people, except punish them. One of Satan's original sins of pride and vanity caused his great fall, and through him and the fallen angels the whole earth was altered. People with Leviathan spirits refuse to apologize, or admit any wrongdoing. It is always the other person's fault.

I don't believe we are to get in agreement with someone who is falsely accusing us, but we should use it as an opportunity to take inventory. We should be willing to look inside ourselves to see if there is any truth in the accusations, what so ever. If there is, we should repent to God and apologize to the person and/or the persons we have offended. **"Agree with thine adversary quickly, while thou art in the way with him, lest at anytime the adversary deliver thee to the judge, and the judge deliver thee to the officer, and thou be cast into prison. Verily I say unto thee, thou shall by no means come out thence, till thou has paid the uttermost farthing." Matthew 5:25-26.** This shows God that we are willing to be humble, and that we are willing to cleanse ourselves and let God be our vindicator. It says to agree while you are in the 'way with him', if you defend yourself using pride, it will become Satan's ace in the hole. He will pull it out and use it against you or cause you to sin against God, often right before you have a breakthrough. Our sins of pride and arrogance give Satan legal right to pull our strings, when it benefits him most. The Bible says that those who curse God's chosen people are 'cursed with a curse'. Since they are already cursed, we mustn't yield to the temptation to curse and revile them back.

The Keys to Victory

Some time into the battle, the evil spirit of Leviathan came to me in a dream, several things were revealed through it, but the most important thing was the spirit looked straight at my husband and me and said, "I am jealous of you, that's why I come to destroy you." I meditated on all the parts of the dream all day, and suddenly the Holy Spirit spoke to my heart and a light bulb came on. The Lord said to my spirit, "Jealousy is the root of the strength that holds Leviathan in place, you must attack and break the spirit of jealousy to uproot the pride," I smiled and thanked the Father for this, knowing now we have the keys to victory! (Our group had just completed another seven day fast, and my dream came to me approximately one AM, just after the fast was officially complete).

The spirit was in the form of a man, the face of the man is someone I know, but he looked like a savage. He was barefoot, half naked, and disheveled. He was in a crouched position that could not stand up. This person is known for his work in the church. His family is full of misogynistic men. In fact, that is their one revelation they stand on. Women must submit! His personality is one of arrogance, misogyny, and pride. While I always liked him, I could always feel that he looked down on me. God had once again caused the enemy to give up its own secrets! Praise to the Most High of Israel, Jesus Christ, and His Holy Spirit! Nothing can compare to His sovereignty! I began to think on these things and realized that Satan's biggest problem was jealousy! **"How art thy fallen from heaven, O Lucifer, son of the morning! How art thou cut down to the ground, which didst weaken the nations! For thou hast said in thine heart, <u>I will ascend into heaven, I will exalt my throne above the stars of God; I will sit also upon the mount of the congregation, in the sides of the North; I will ascend above the heights of the clouds; I will be like the Most High</u>." Isaiah 14:12-15**

The definition of jealous is this: 1. Resentment against a rival, a person enjoying success or advantage, or against another's success of advantage itself. 2. Mental uneasiness from suspicion or fear of rivalry. 3. Vigilance in maintaining or guarding something.

Jealousy and its nature are controlling and defiling. Have you ever noticed when you are around someone who is jealous of you, it feels like you have been 'slimed'? It is important to pray and break off the defilement brought on by jealousy from others. Because of my past dealings with this evil spirit, I try to make it important to allow everyone to function in his or her spiritual and natural gifts and help nourish them in our church. Persons who have pride perceive your gifts as a threat to them. The Bible gives us clear instruction about how the body of Christ should look. **"For the body is not one member, but many. If the foot shall say, because I am not the hand, I am not of the body; it is therefore not of the body? 1 Corinthians 20:15. "But now are they many members, yet but one body. And the eye cannot say unto the hand, I have no need of thee; nor again the head to the feet; I have no need of thee." 1 Corinthians 20:21.** The false kingdom of Ahab, Jezebel, and Leviathan want to control the congregation. They only want like-minded people in their clichés. (My dear friend remarked to me that she believes they try to emulate the trinity. Jezebel wants to be God, Ahab obeys her like Jesus obeys the Father, and I have always know that Leviathan is the counterfeit of the Holy Spirit. It's something to think about, huh?)

In this way our churches are distorted, people show up, sit in the pew, write a check, and go home. If you are not a singer, musician, or nursery worker you are not needed. Nothing more is allowed or required, so people become Luke-warm and disengaged. I am not saying that we should let the tail wag the dog, but every person has a part to play. Every person has a gift to give, even if it is just a gift of zeal or excitement for the Lord. Everyone has worth in the true church. Unless they are wolves, we should love, respect, and nurture their gifts and callings, not destroy them.

My husband and I went to a non-denominational church several years ago, they had so many rules and regulations, and I could not keep up. I brought a young lady with me one Sunday and went to the altar with her. The pastor's wife always sat on the stage on her "throne", and she came down and prayed for the girl I had brought. While she was praying, I put my arm around my friend. After church was dismissed, I was met at the door by an elder and rebuked. He said, "We do not allow anyone to touch others at our altar." I thought to myself, " I am the one that brought her here, but okay." The next Sunday, I brought a toddler with us and took her to the nursery. After praise and worship, I went to the restroom and peeked in the window of the nursery to check on the baby. After service an elder met me again at the door. Apparently, I wasn't allowed to do that either. I apologized and told him I didn't know all of the rules.

Week after week something like this happened, I just couldn't do anything right! We went one night and they had an evangelist speaking. He was very much anointed and his message was awesome. However, at the altar call he came down the aisle, and pointed at my husband and me, and began to prophesy over us. His prophecy was about what is happening right now, we received it and sat back down. The next Sunday we were met with such hostility by the people, especially the Pastor's wife and daughter, you would have thought we had the plague. That was okay, we had gotten what we were supposed to get from the evangelist, and we moved on. To this day, no one called to check on us, which is fine by me, but looking back I realized that this man's family controlled the entire church. His wife was lifted up in almost every sermon. The pastor would even say that the Holy Spirit's voice sounded to him like his wife's voice. His daughter was the church secretary and praise and worship leader.

The rest of the praise team consisted of his son, son in law, and daughter in law. Talk about controlling, my goodness! This one took the cake. I have dubbed that church as the most hateful church I have ever seen. It cracks me up because they have a big billboard in the town where they are that says their name and under it says something like this, "Come and feel the love of God." I didn't get hurt over this treatment at all; in fact, I was sort of used to it. Now that is just sad. I wonder how many other sheep have been mistreated and wounded. I wonder what Judgment Day is going to look like for these so called shepherds?

Is it possible that jealousy was roused because the out of town prophet called us out and prophesied to us that we would have our own ministry and pull things down from the heavenlies that would change many lives? Yes. I think so. Instead of trying to support us, get to know us, or shepherd us, we were treated like dirt. Isn't that strange? What spirit were they listening to? You will remember that Cain slew Abel because of jealousy. He was jealous of him because God honored Abel's offering over his own. Instead of taking correction and going back and saying, "How can I please God?" He committed murder. He killed his own flesh and blood and even had the nerve to be arrogant towards God saying, "Am I my brother's keeper?" Now if that isn't pride born of jealousy, then I don't what is! The same happens today, those who do not understand your gift, say it isn't real, because they don't have it. They 'murder' you and make you small. Instead of asking God, what shall I do for you Lord? They covet and devour.

I have four brothers, all are successful, one very wealthy, but my third brother is a humble truck driver. He uses his time on the road to call and check on the family. We call him the information officer because he keeps up with us all. However, God has used him mightily in my life. I have talked to him for years about ministry and the Lord. He is like a sounding board for me. But the most unique thing he does for me, is this, he speaks wisdom. Sometimes when he speaks, I feel as if God himself is speaking to me. He is the least educated of us all, and by all accounts a simple man. But his gift has helped me tremendously. He not only encourages me, he also corrects me. It is done from a place of unconditional love, and I am very thankful for him. He has never made me feel small or stupid for being a girl or for serving the Lord. He has been a source of support for me that I believe is a gift from God. So when correction comes forth through him, I perk up and listen. I believe if I had got in pride and overthrew him with my knowledge, I would not be where I am today. He is one of many wise people God has put in my life. I am not a detail person; sometimes I don't see the trees because I'm focused on the forest, or the big picture. We need people in our lives that can minister truth to us, no matter who we are. I need the detail people; you may need the big picture person. I say again, all God's true children have tremendous worth in the kingdom.

I am sure many of you have been treated the same way in church as we have been. It is very discouraging and causes you to feel rejected and alone. I am here to tell you that you are not alone. Use it as an opportunity to check your inventory, if you are truly out of line, repent. But do not stay in a church that mistreats and reviles you. Jesus addressed this in the Bible. **"All therefore whatsoever they bid you observe and do; do not ye after their works (don't act like them.) For they say, and do not. For they bind heavy burdens and grievous to be borne, and lay them on men's shoulders; but they themselves will not move with them one of their fingers" Matthew 23:4.** In other words, in their pride, they want to tell you how to act and behave but are unwilling to do themselves what they require of you. They are totally unwilling to help you come out of the bondage they accuse you of having. As a shepherd and leader, we must be the first to deal with our sins before pointing out the sins others. We must never think we are above correction, if do we are in pride. **"Blessed are the meek, for they shall inherit the earth." Matthew 5:5.**

King David explains it best in Psalms. **"Lord, my heart is not haughty, nor mine eyes lofty; neither do I exercise myself in great matters or in things to high for me." Psalms131: 1.** Even though he was called by God and carried a huge anointing, he understood that haughtiness would destroy him. He was described as 'a man after God's own heart'. He was concerned with his relationship with God and not his station in life. He sinned and transgressed against God, but he also walked with God in humility, seeming to understand that it was the Father and His Majesty that was worthy of worship and praise, not his many accomplishments or kingdom. I see him as a man that understood repentance, and had a healthy fear of God. In fact, we read the scriptures in Psalms in many of our deliverance sessions. They are powerful warfare prayers, and demons hate them.

Many years ago I cast the spirit of self-importance out of myself. I asked the Lord to help me understand humility. I saw a vision of Jesus hanging on the cross, it was in the distance, but his head was hung low and his body was limp. I wept and wept. How could I possibly understand that kind of humility? After twenty years of walking with the Lord, I still cannot grasp the fullness of it. It will be a lifelong pursuit for us, in our walk with God. It should be in the foremost of our prayers, it should be the desire of our heart. **"(For my determined purpose is) that I may know him (that I may progressively become more deeply and intimately acquainted with him, perceiving and recognizing and understanding the wonders of HIS person more strongly and more clearly), and that I may in the same way come to know the power out flowing from HIS resurrection (which exerts over believers), and that I may so share HIS sufferings as to be continually transformed (in spirit into HIS likeness even unto HIS death in the hope that if possible I may attain to the spiritual and moral resurrections that lifts me) out from among the dead (even while in the body)" Philippians 3:10-11 Amplified**

Chapter Eight: Kingdom of Babylon

"Behold, the days come, that all that is in thine house, and that which thy fathers have laid up store unto this day, shall be left, saith the Lord. And thy sons that shall take issue from thee, which thou shall begat, shall they take away; and they shall be eunuchs (neutered slaves/ servants) in the palace of the Kingdom of Babylon". 2 Kings20: 17-18.

What great sin had God's people committed for them to be punished so severly? To be given over to a heathen nation as slaves? They turned away from serving God and obeying him and had begun serving other gods. **"And go not after other gods to serve them, and to worship them, and provoke me not to anger with the works of your hands; and I will do you no harm. Yet ye have not hearkened to me, saith the Lord; that ye might provoke me to anger with works of your hands to your own hurt. There thus saith the Lord of hosts; because ye have not heard my words, Behold I will send and take all the families of the north, saith the Lord, and Nebuchadnezzar, the King of Babylon…" Jeremiah 25:6-9.**

The root word for Babylon means "confusion (by mixing)". When the Holy Spirit is snuffed out and other spirits rule it breeds confusion! Confusion keeps people from hearing, obeying, and fully serving God. It is common and accepted for Christians to consult horoscopes, psychics, partake in hypnosis, and the like. I have heard some psychics claim they are 'Christian'. We cannot put a cross on our occultic practices and expect God to be okay with it. We cannot do as our forefathers did and say we serve The Most High God, but then follow the doctrines of demons! We are in covenant with Him. When we serve pride, anger, jealousy, and the like, we are not serving God. In your natural marriage, would you want your spouse to date or court other people? I know I would not! We cannot expect God to be any different. The first two, out of the Ten Commandments are these: 1. Thou shall have no other Gods before me 2. Thou shall not make unto thee any graven image, or likeness of anything that is in heaven above, or that is in the earth beneath, or that is in the water and the earth. You shall not bow down and serve them, for I the Lord, am a jealous God visiting the iniquity of the fathers on the children.

This is exactly what sentenced Saul to death. **"Then Saul said unto his servants, seek me a woman that hath a familiar spirit that I may go to her and inquire of her." 1 Samuel 28:7.** The witch of Endor conjured up a spirit and it prophesied doom over Saul. **"So Saul died for his transgression which he committed against the Lord, even against the word of the Lord, which he kept not, and also for asking counsel of one that had a familiar spirit, to inquire of it; and inquired not of the Lord; therefore he slew him, and turned the kingdom unto David, the son of Jesse" 1 Chronicles 10:13.** We have a God in heaven to whom we must seek for answers, but that requires obedience and love. We must dwell with Him in knowledge and reverential fear. His will should be the answers we long for, not our own.

I believe the spirits of Ahab, Jezebel, and Leviathan are the enforcers and have successfully set up the kingdom of Babylon. The true manna from heaven is rarely received because God's people are confused. We are confused about the nature of God and His Holy Spirit; we are confused about Jesus Christ and what he died to give us! Look at the many denominations of the churches, none of them can agree! All stubbornly believe they are right! The body of Christ is more divided than ever. We just simply cannot get into unity with one another! **"They will not frame their doings to turn unto their God, for the spirit of whoredoms is in the midst of them, and they have not known the Lord." Hosea 5:4.**

"For where envy and strife is, there is <u>confusion</u> and every evil work" James 3:16. While churches compete with one another, one trying to outdo the other, the innocent sheep are being slaughtered and scattered. This is why my husband and I refrained from speaking against the local churches. We wanted to be part of the solution, not part of the problem. Scripture tells us that the kingdom of Babylon will finally be overthrown. **"And there followed another angel, saying, Babylon is fallen, is fallen, that great city, because she made <u>all</u> nations drink of the wrath of her fornication" Revelations 14:8.**

The children of Israel were handed over to the Babylonians for following false gods. I fear the church had done the same. Stephen speaks of this in the scripture. **"Yea, you took up the tabernacle of Moloch, and the star of your god Remphan, figures which ye made to worship them: and I will carry you away beyond Babylon" Acts 7:43.** Notice that this was the chosen people, in covenant with God that "made" and set up these false gods. It is the same in the church today. We have sold ourselves into captivity. We have sinned against God! We would rather spend time with our 'idols' than to spend time with Him! We honor him with our lips but our hearts are far from Him. **"This people draweth nigh unto me with their mouth, and honor me with their lips; but their heart is far from me" Matthew 15:8**

Jesus called these people hypocrites, and he was speaking to the leaders of the synagogues (the church). The root word of hypocrite means "an actor". He spoke to their heart condition, saying outwardly they looked clean, but inwardly they were filthy, and their filthiness was polluting God's people. We as leaders will be judged with double judgment. We have to get clean FIRST! Will you search your heart and humble yourself before God? No matter what size congregation you have or how big your salary and recognition is, will you become like the least esteemed and repent? Are you willing to do as King David did, and sit upon your bed and commune with your heart? (Psalms 4:4). Will you get clean? (Job 9:30) Will you fight the good fight of faith and take your city for God? (1 Timothy 6:12).

We see in the Old Testament that when God's people sinned against Him and served other gods, he would turn them over to Babylon. **"And they slew the sons of Zedekiah (the King of Judah) before his eyes, and put out the eyes of Zedekiah, and bound him with fetters of brass, and carried him to Babylon.... and he burnt the house of the Lord, and the King's house, and all the houses of Jerusalem, and every great man's house burnt he with fire. And the army of the Chaldeans, that were with the captain of the guard, broke down the walls of Jerusalem round about" 2 Kings 25:7**

The prophet Jeremiah was born for such day. The Lord called him and sanctified him in his mother's womb to be a true prophet to Israel. He was told by God to prophesy to the king and to the people that if they did not repent, and put away their idols, that they would be given over to Babylon as slaves, and the temple and city would be destroyed and burned. They did not listen to him; in fact they beat him, tortured him, and locked him away. But every word he spoke came to pass. They chose to listen to the false prophet Hananiah. Hananiah would die within the year, just as Jeremiah had proclaimed, yet the king still refused to hear him. Why did the king prefer the false prophet to the true? Because the false prophet will tell you what you want to hear. He will stroke you, and speak soothing words of peace and prosperity to you. He does not love the truth; therefore he will not seek the truth for you. And if we follow him, we will end up as captives and slaves to the kingdom of Babylon.

Jeremiah is known as the 'weeping prophet'. He did not want to speak these things, and he knew they would not hear him. He knew they would abuse him, but God promised him that although they would fight against him, they would not prevail against him. **"For I am with you, saith the Lord, to deliver thee." Jeremiah 1:19.** While Jeremiah's life was certainly hard, imagine his status today in heaven and in eternity! He was hated for God, but LOVED by God!

I wrote this a few years ago about Jeremiah:

"I have been meditating on the plight of Jeremiah, aka the weeping prophet, and seemingly he was born in a time of great turmoil. The people of Israel, the people in covenant, were very wicked and Jeremiah was for born for this time in history. Jeremiah chapter one describes how God had separated him from his mother's womb and consecrated him to be a true prophet to the people of Israel and the nations. He then tells him that the whole land would fight against him but would not prevail. Do you ever feel that way? I know I do!

The people said, **"Let us devise devices against Jeremiah, for the law shall not perish from the priest, or counsel from the wise, or the word of the prophet. Come, let us smite him with the tongue, and let us not give heed to any of his words" Jeremiah 18:18.** What they meant was, we are holier than him, and we have our priests and prophets. We don't have to listen to this guy. He is nobody. Though everything he spoke was true and they refused to repent. They knew he was of God and they chose the false!

In chapter 20, Jeremiah is now in prison being beaten, and he cries out, **"For since I spoke (for God), I cried out, I cried violence and spoil; because the word of the Lord has made a reproach unto me and a derision daily.** Then he said, **"I will not make mention of Him anymore, nor speak His name. But His word was in my heart as a burning fire shut up in my bones, and I was weary with forbearing, and I could not**

stay (keep quiet)". Does this sound familiar to you? It should! In verse 14 he says, **"Cursed be the day; let not the day my mother bare me to be blessed".** He was so persecuted and discouraged, that he wished he were never born! Jeremiah lived on and saw his prophesies fulfilled. His life was full of torment, mockery, and abuse but I guarantee you his status in heaven is probably very great. Don't grow weary saints, our Lord is worth it!

I fear we are living in a much direr situation than even Jeremiah saw. I believe we are living as slaves to the kingdom of Babylon more than ever! Just as it was in Jeremiah's day, it is God's chosen people who have set up the kingdom to fall into the hands of the enemy. The temple of God was destroyed because it had become a den of devils. The one true God was being 'mixed' with the demonic pagan gods, and the people of God somehow thought that it was okay. Even a person familiar with doing laundry will tell you that you cannot mix dark colored clothing with white clothing. The dark will bleed over into the white and ruin it. We will throw the garment away or use it for dust rags. It is no longer sharp, white and clean, it is tainted. The temple was destroyed twice and we wait for it to be built for the third time now. That is one of our final signs that the Lord is returning soon. As I referenced earlier, the spiritual kingdom of Babylon will not be completely overthrown until Christ returns. (See Revelations14: 8, 10, and 21).

That doesn't mean we can't overthrow Babylon in our midst today. In fact, we must overthrow it in our homes, our churches, and in the heavenlies. Listen to the "Jeremiah's" in place today! Rise up and proclaim truth to God's people. We are called to be salt, not sugar. Salt purifies. When placed in a wound, it burns, but also cleanses. Sugar makes the people grow fat, and we come addicted to its sweetness. We must get clean, purified, and purged for the kingdom to come. God is not looking for a spoiled, fat, pampered church. He is looking for a church making themselves ready. Taking correction and humbling ourselves to Him. He does not want us mixing truth with the pagan, demonic gods of pride, selfishness, and love of money. He did not look the other way in the past, and he will not do so now. It is time we put the Lord back on the throne. To do that, we must cleanse our hands and hearts. **"The Lord rewarded me accordingly to my righteousness; according to the cleanness of my hands in His eyesight." Psalms 18:20.**

The prophet Daniel describes God's people in the last days as those that are 'tried, purged, and made white'. Your church attendance record and tithe offerings won't be the issue. Your obedience and willingness to resist the devil, and submit to God, will be the key to weathering the turbulent times we may face, and are already facing. If you are willing, He will walk with you in doing these things. He will guide you and lead you into the way of truth. He will make a way for you!

Chapter Nine: Jezebel, the Cunning

At the beginning of this battle, as I said before, I was able to actually see the spirit realm clearly. But just as I could see them in the beginning, they could see me as well. At one point a lady contacted me on Face book. She is a self-proclaimed witch, but was also a relative of one of my dearest friends. I allowed her to be my friend on Facebook, in hopes that God could somehow reach her. I felt she was harmless. I love her and pray for her when I see her online. On my page she wrote " Angela, please be careful... you are very blessed." To which I responded, "Don't worry, I am being very careful", She replied back," They can see you and feel you." I said back, "Yes I know. I know they know who I am."

I sat back and smiled, because I knew from past experience that this was a good thing. You cannot engage what you cannot see. The next day in prayer, I saw a vision of the woman, she was in her kitchen furiously stirring something in a pot, and she looked up at me, bared her teeth and growled. I knew she was angry with herself for alerting me, I believe she was probably being attacked because of it, and I felt she was casting spells against me. I prayed for her and bound and blinded the eyes of the occultists, I prayed for their souls. That's when I knew to pray To God to hide us from their "senses".

When my friend asked her sister about this and what she had meant, she played dumb, and said she didn't know what she was talking about. This was the first indicator to me that God was going to cause the enemy to be so confused, that they would essentially give up their own secrets. A week or so later, I was at a charity fundraiser, an acquaintance of ours, who knew nothing about our ministry approached me and said, " Angie, have you heard about all the Satanist moving here recently?" I told her no, I hadn't, but I wasn't surprised. She said 'Well, They need to GO!" I thought to myself, you have no idea how right you are! It seemed logical to me that Jezebel was rousing and sending her witches to our county. Anytime God is doing something, the enemy is sent forth to try and stop it. We are determined that this time, they will be defeated.

Jezebel was the High Priestess of the cult of Ashtoreth, and she not only worshiped Ashtoreth, but also she was determined to murder and destroy all of God's true prophets. We see in 1 Kings Chapter 18 that Jezebel sends for Elijah to kill him. She and Ahab had already killed many of Gods prophets and leaders. Thankfully through the obedience of Obadiah, he had hidden seven thousand true prophets in caves. It is said that they had not 'bowed' to the Baal's. The kingdom of Jezebel and Ahab have murdered and killed the prophets of God for centuries, even after Jesus ascended to heaven.

"And I saw the woman drunken with the blood of the saints, and with the blood of the martyrs of Jesus: and when I saw her I wondered with great admiration." Revelation 17:6

"And in her was found the blood of the prophets, and of the saints, and of all that were slain upon the earth." Revelation 18:24

Jezebel is a murdering spirit with fear and death as her servants. She will continue to kill us unless we kill her first. But we must overthrow Ahab and Leviathan! Her power comes from them, so they must be recognized and subdued before we can see victory over Jezebel.

Jezebel is the queen of all witchcrafts, but her greatest accomplishment has been in deceiving and seducing God's chosen people. There is much written about her, and many sermons available online about her and the way she attacks. But very few about the two demons her give her power, Ahab and Leviathan. We know, without a shadow of a doubt, that you have to overthrow them before you can ever touch Jezebel. Ahab gives her authority and Leviathan gives her strength. To try and engage her without defeating these two will leave you feeling hopeless and worn down. It is she that sets up the Baal's. Let's look at what she did to the prophet Elijah.

God had sent a famine to the land through the word of Elijah. **"And Elijah the Tishbite, who was of the inhabitants of Gilead, said unto Ahab, As the Lord GOD of Israel liveth, before whom I stand, there shall not be dew nor rain these years, but according to my word"1 Kings 17:1.** God then sends him to a brook where he is fed bread and meat by way of ravens, when the brook dried up, God sent him to a widow's house and miraculously provided for the prophet, the widow and her household. Elijah walked in the gift of miracles. One barrel of meal and one bottle of oil lasted them the remainder of the famine. The woman's son however became sick and died. The prophet laid him across a bed and lay on top of him, after praying three times, the child came back to life. God was affirming to Elijah that he was with him. He was preparing him psychologically for the next phase of his ministry.

The Bible says after many days had passed, Elijah went before Ahab to show himself as Gods messenger. **"And it came to pass, when Ahab saw Elijah, that Ahab, said unto him, Art thou he that troubles Israel? And he answered, I have not troubled Israel, but thou, and thy fathers house, in that ye have forsaken the commandments of the Lord, and thou hast followed Baalim. Now therefore send, and gather to me all Israel unto Mount Carmel, and the priests of Baal four hundred and fifty, and the prophets of the groves four hundred, which eat at Jezebel's table". 1 Kings 18:19**

There he confronted the false prophets and made mockery of them. They could not call fire down from heaven with their powers, though they tried all day long to do so.

Scripture tells us 'they cried aloud, and cut themselves with knives and lancets, till the blood gushed out of them", but still there gods could not speak. Elijah stood and challenged them, saying, whomevers God would answer and send fire down from heaven, was indeed the one true God. When he had ordered them to soak the wood with water three times, he prayed to the God of Abraham, Isaac and Jacob, then fire fell, and consumed the wood and the stones and the dust and licked up the water that was in the trench. When the people saw this they humbled themselves, fell on their faces and repented, saying, "The Lord, He is God, The Lord, He is God"! Elijah told them to gather all the false prophets and kill them. As soon as this was done a cloud arose up and a great rain fell, thus showing that God alone had the power to end the famine. This mighty act of God would stir up Jezebels wrath and she would unleash her powers of witchcraft against Elijah to the point that he ran from her in fear. You will recall that our experience at Red River had shown us about the fear that comes through witchcraft. We had been shown not to give fear any place while doing warfare; we knew that was the main weapon they use. Another point I want to make about Jezebel is that she is very persistent. She doesn't give up easily, she will attempt to wear you out, make you feel depressed, and even doubt your ability to overcome her. No principality or power in heaven or on earth can defeat Our God, but she will sure make you think that she can. I do not want you to think I am making light of her powers. I am merely telling you that the blood of Jesus decimates her, and the Father has granted us authority in His son's name to stand against her and every vile unclean thing. One of the words God spoke to me in the beginning stages of this battle is found in The last part of Philippians 3 **"'...according to the working whereby he (Jesus) is able to subdue all things unto himself."**

In Revelation chapter 2:20 Jesus shows John that the church was still tolerating the Jezebelian spirit, **"Not withstanding, I have a few things against thee, because thou suffereth that woman Jezebel, which calleth herself a prophetess, to teach and to seduce my servants to commit fornication, and to eat things sacrificed to idols. And I gave her space to repent of her fornication; and she repented not. Behold I will cast her into a (sick) bed, and them that commit adultery with her into great tribulation, except they repent of their deeds. And I will kill her children with death; and all the churches shall know he which searches the reins and hearts: and I will give unto every one of you according to your works." Revelation 2:20-23.**

The word Jezebel means "cannot co-habitate." We cannot live with her and have peace. Those who are infected with her can have no peace. She is called by Satan to murder God's people. She is trying to kill us, and she is succeeding!

This scripture alone reveals much about her influence and power in the Church. She is called a false prophetess that teaches and seduces Gods servants to commit fornication. Fornication is the same as spiritual adultery. We are called the Bride of Christ. When we serve Jezebel and eat from her table, we are sinning greatly against God. People with the Jezebel spirit often have infirmities, many will have female problems. It is my belief that is where she resides, in the reproductive organs. When praying for women who have this spirit, they state every single time that their womb hurts. I had a similar experience with my own body.

I will give you an example of how she works., My favorite church to date was a victim of and an example to me of how these spirits operate and take over a whole church. A husband and wife that we had known for awhile invited us. The man was a man of wealth, he was older by the time we met him, and he was a great supporter of our ministry. They had been a part, briefly of the false deliverance ministry I spoke of earlier, and the husband had broke ties with them. His wife however kept a relationship with them, going on vacation with the man's wife every year, and called her 'daughter.' She spent money on them behind her husband's back. In fact, when I would go shopping with her, she would lie to him about how much money she spent.

She was addicted to shopping, and would leave things in the trunk of her car to keep her husband from seeing them. She always dressed to kill, wearing very high heels and jewelry in excess. This brought her much attention, because she was in her late sixties. Her lying always bothered me, but I felt it was none of my business. She talked of the Lord constantly, but it was always the same repetitive, vague statements. She appeared to be totally in love with God. She took great delight in Church and always carried her Bible. She always talked about how she was raised in a godly home. She made everyone feel like she had some type of special access to The Lord. People flocked to her for advice and counsel. My discernment told me that she was deceived in many ways, but I loved her deeply.

Not long after we started going to Church with them, her husband became gravely ill and died. Soon after he died, I would witness with my own eyes her transformation into a full-blown Jezebel.

I had begun having women's ministry in our church. We only met once a month, so I had plenty of time to pray about each message, which I did. The teachings were of the milkiest of the milk, but people were getting blessed, and some were coming to the altar for prayer. The woman was happy and beaming with pride at first. (I found out later that she took credit for my sermons, telling one lady that I would consult her and get my teachings from her.)

The Lord had put it upon my heart to teach on the spiritual gifts in 1 Corinthians 12. It was (in my mind) a very basic teaching, but deeper than I had done before. I noticed commotion in the back and saw her arguing furiously with another woman. She was agitated and upset. I am not sure exactly when but preceding this, I had a dream. I was standing in the sanctuary of the Church, dressed in a white robe, the Holy Spirit said, "Look daughter". Suddenly, I saw a large octopus with the face of the woman, only her mouth was on the side of her face and she was speaking slander. She rose up in the air and began spinning; her tentacles were going out and landing on the tops of people's heads. It went deep into some, and others it would just rest lightly.

When I awoke, The Lord said, "This is the nature of Jezebel, she controls the minds of my people, and slanders God's true prophets, just as she is now slandering you". Some days later I spoke to the pastor about it, He admitted to me that she had came to him complaining after my last teaching, saying I was trying to bring tongues into our Church. This was a lie. I had spoken on all the gifts and didn't give any certain one more significance than the other (though I believe in them all). I warned Him about the dream and also shared with him other things that God had showed me were about to take place.

I now know, that she was plotting to bring Leviathan in, and did so shortly after. She had to get rid of me first, and she knew it. I was very surprised the Pastor let him in. He had victimized him too in the past. I did not know that the pastor was her Ahab. Sadly, Jezebel and Leviathan are ruling completely now. People tell me that it is just a circus over there now, a big social club. I still pray for them to this day, because many innocent sheep are being harmed and led astray. The Lord showed me that the Pastors love of money was the cause of his fall. I was sad because I believe when we first met him; he had a true desire for God. I begged God for him and the Lord said to me, "He has never wanted to be serious about me, so I have given him over to the desires of his heart."

This has taught me that we cannot give Jezebel any power, because it is power that she lusts for. Money is just a tool. To her, it is status, influence and control that she craves. I was told that they frequently lift her up from the pulpit and praise her. I know the pastor gets money from her; in fact we got sucked into doing that too for a while. My husband gave him $125 a week for several months, and even pushed for him to get a large raise. But as soon as he didn't agree with him on a matter of great importance, my husband was literally thrown under the bus. There was blatant sin in the leadership at the time. Some of the young people's marriages were in jeopardy and we felt we needed to help them, counsel them, love them and restore. My husband as an elder would get multiple calls weekly from the congregants about a particular fellow. He felt he had to do something. He was met with extreme anger from the pastor; the other elders agreed with him to his face but stabbed him in the back in front of the whole church. I felt so bad for him, he had been used to get the pastor a raise and other things and as soon as he disagreed with him he was put on display and mocked.

The young man who was having the problem would be divorced within a year. Instead of asking him to step down temporarily from leadership, and helping him, he was thrown to the wolves. But this hurt many people. The Jezebel spirit had her hand in this too. She was one of the biggest complainers about this young man, pressuring my husband to do something about him almost daily. The night that it went before the Church, she was strangely absent. A lady friend of mine overheard her the very next day talking to the man's aunt. She was blaming us and said she had nothing to do with it.

That day I got four phone calls from random people telling me that she was slandering me and accusing me of outrageous things. My heart broke and I wept, because she had been my friend, and I loved her. Today I am thankful God delivered me from her. Though she could never control me, she did have influence in my life. If I had not had a strong backbone and a personal relationship with God, I could have easily been one of her eunuchs or children, as she has many.

A month or so after I left the church, I had a chance encounter with one of the women who I had seen in the dream, the tentacles had sunk deep into her head. She began to speak to me in a confusing angry tone. I finally asked her, "What exactly are you rebuking me for; I can't make sense of what you're saying?" She answered that she knew that I had gotten all my sermons from the Jezebel woman, and that I was not of God. I said," I prayed and sought the Lord before every teaching, you have been deceived. Why are you so viscously attacking me?" She became so confused and began to stammer. She was being used by Jezebel and was acting as her Ashtoreth. To this day, she is sickly and in tribulation. That is the fruit of submitting to Jezebel.

Here are some of these evil spirits characteristics:

* She attaches herself to men with wealth, she is a gold digger.
* She uses flattery and seduction, when need be to accomplish her agenda.
* She often looks super spiritual, but it is false. Look at her fruit.
* She is either hyper sexual or frigid towards her husband. She will use sex to manipulate him.
* She can be outwardly controlling or can be subtle about it (example: self pity is common in the subtle Jezebel). Whatever it takes to get her way.
* She wants recognition for all her works, "Look at me, Look at me."
* She uses her eyes to seduce and curse others. I have seen the cold blank stare of her and the seductive eyes of flattery both when casting her out.
* If you confront her, no matter how humbly, she will stiffen up and cock her head. This too happens every time I have confronted her in prayer.

* The most powerful Jezebels have covens of like-minded people that do her bidding; in this way she teaches them and incites them to rebellion.

* She has a gift of mind control, even projecting thoughts into the minds of others.

* Jezebel in women despises authority and teaches their daughters to be 'man haters'. She will undermine them at every turn, while smiling at their face and flattering them, she is a back stabber.

* Seeks to emasculate the males in her life, they are to be made into her Eunuchs.

* She is very self-centered and talks about herself nonstop, draining and wearying everyone around her.

* She loves to say, "thus saith The Lord ", but her prophecies never come to pass.

* In the home she is the Queen Bee, and uses matriarchal control over her husband and children. Since he feels less spiritual than her, he allows her to lead the family.

* She is bossy in nature, and will lie in a heartbeat to cover her tracks.

* She is over protective of her natural children, and rules them. She expects others to bow down to them as well. In this way she kills them spiritually. They are her idols.

* When they are grown, she refuses to cut the apron strings and allow them to be accountable to God; everything they do is ok, though she has very high standards for others. She makes excuses for them. If she has sons, they will be expected to serve the daughters. This ensures the matriarchal kingdom will be passed on.

* If she has sons, they will be made into "mama's boys."

* She is a perfectionist, with high standards, but they do not apply to her, only others.
* She will sob and cry, shout and scream to try and get you to submit to her, we must not fear her or feel sorry for her.
* She is a slave to fashion, and wants to dress to kill. (I don't believe women should wear potato sacks, but modesty and balance is key). Subtle Jezebels' may go the other extreme, looking plain and dowdy.
* Look for confusing speech; this is part of her witchcraft. She speaks in riddles and confusion, never getting to the point.
* She will use slander to attempt to destroy anyone who opposes her, just as she did with Naboth.

I feel I must undo the stigma and taboo regarding the word Jezebel. Movies and churches portray her as a harlot. I assure you, that can be a fruit of the Jezebel spirit, but when I was getting free from the spirit, I realized that she feels like extreme anxiety. This spirit has Gods daughters so anxious that we walk around in a cycle of fear, anxiety and stress. She also gives demonic visions, which induces stress. For example, I would lie down at night and a vision of someone I loved being harmed or in an accident would flood my mind. I would sit up in bed and refute the false visions and tell her to leave. Daughters of God must feel safe enough to come to us and get help and deliverance from Jezebel. I want to encourage you to do just that. This spirit has put her tentacles into all of us, and if left unchecked she will destroy us, emotionally, physically and spiritually. While I had skipped right through the Ahab and Leviathan deliverance and watched others struggle with those, when it came time to deal with Jezebel, I was stunned and deeply grieved that the evil spirit had used me too in my life. God began showing us how to get free from her. I had a dream and God began revealing to me that through wounds and traumas, I had darkness in my heart. These were the breaches that allowed her to have access to me. One by one the Lord would allow a wound to surface. Each time I would feel the pain, cry and confess it to someone (usually my husband) and then I would feel the Holy Spirit envelope me and the pain and sadness would leave. I could physically feel this happening. Not long after, the Lord began doing the same thing to the other ladies in the group. This happened for about a month and then suddenly the Lord began to deliver me from the underling spirits of Jezebel. As I was getting prayer, I saw what seemed like a movie, or my life flashing before my eyes. God was showing me instances where I had operated in this unclean spirit. I flung myself to the ground and began repenting and begging God to help me. It was the most intense deliverance I have ever personally experienced. I realized that it would take time to break habits and mindsets that were familiar to me, especially in the areas of anxiety. I know I have to guard my heart against this spirit, as I believe she is assigned primarily to females. The next service I had, the anointing was so strong in me that people could physically see and feel it. I felt it too, and realized that the Jezebel spirit had most definitely affected my anointing. I was disciplined enough to walk in the spirit most of the time, but I would often get to a point of frustration and anxiety about the ministry. This was her working. I am determined to close every breach in my heart that gives her access. My goal is to see every single woman set free from her tentacles. After my personal deliverance, I began to walk in a super natural peace that I have never felt. After 23 years of marriage, my husband and I feel like newlyweds without these evil spirits in our midst. It is a true miracle.

People with Jezebel spirits often were rejected and traumatized by a male authority figure, which in turn causes rebellion. **"For rebellion is as the sin of witchcraft, and stubbornness is as iniquity and idolatry" Samuel 15: 23.** She seeks the wounded, and succeeds easily with people who have been victimized. It is through broken hearts that she gains access. She also can get passed on through generational sins. Since Jezebel is modeled to us while growing up, the person will take on their ways by way of example. God's daughters have been overlooked and mistreated for so many generations that this is the result of that sin. The sins have piled up, and the manifestation in the natural is total confusion. I haven't heard one preacher (including myself) that has it all right. Men and women are either overbearing, or too passive. We will not find the balance until we deal with these demons. Homosexuality is on the rise, transgender people, and ADHD in children are just a few things that stem from this false kingdom. The abortion movement also falls under this curse.

God gave Jezebel time and space to repent. Since many of them are so wounded inside, you may have to minister and pray healing for them first. The first step they have to take is to forgive. We can and should have mercy for the person, but we can show no mercy towards this spirit. If you are insecure or easily swayed, you will not defeat Jezebel. The goal is to facilitate freedom, healing and deliverance for the person, not to shame them, attack them or condone Jezebel. This only keeps the person in bondage longer. True shepherds will always work harder for the sheep than the sheep work for them, however, if the person isn't willing to change, we cannot make them. Many times we will have to let them go. I humbled myself to the woman I spoke of before and even got on my knees before her and spoke to her, like a daughter to a mother because she is older than me. Her back stiffened, she cocked her head, and became as hard as a stone and laughed right in my face. I had no choice but to remove her from my life. Though I still pray for her, we have no contact what so ever.

"And Ahab told Jezebel all that Elijah had done, and withal how he had slain all the prophets with the sword. Then Jezebel sent a messenger unto Elijah, saying, so let the gods do to me, and also

more, if I make not thy life as the life of one of them by tomorrow about this time. And when he (Elijah) saw that he arose, and went for his life, and came to Beer Sheba, which belonged to Judah, and left his servant there. But he himself went a day's journey into the wilderness, and came and sat down under a juniper tree: and he requested for himself that he might die; and he said, it is enough O Lord, take away my life; for I am no better than my fathers." 1 Kings 19:1-4

When battling Jezebel, expect to feel despair, depressed and fearful. These thoughts would come to my entire group and me. I would have to pray and bind her witchcrafts from the group constantly. Then my neck would hurt, I prayed and the Lord showed me it was another attack from her. As soon as we prayed against it, it would stop. For several days in a row, I would get so cold. I could feel a cold breeze blowing through the house. I even checked the thermostat thinking the air conditioning was on. I mentioned it to another member of the group, and he said he had been feeling the same way. I knelt and prayed, and I saw a vision of lips blowing frigid air at me. I have no idea why. We also battled constant infirmities. Nausea, headaches, body aches, you name it. There was no way we could get complacent. Her attacks were going to back fire on her; it was just a matter of time. Until my group and I were completely cleansed of her or any spirits that sympathized with her, God was going to let us feel her.

Some preachers teach that she causes car accidents and other catastrophes. We had none of that, but again we were vigilant in prayer and fasting. When one of us would get down, another would be up. This is why having a dependable mature leadership team is so important. We had to be very transparent, and confess our sins constantly. Every service almost, someone was getting prayer. It got very tiresome. I would fall into bed every night exhausted and wake up just as tired. The people needed me to be strong for them, and God was counting on all of our obedience.

It was not fun, and will not be fun for you. But it is necessary, and vitally important. Even if only one person is set free, it is worth it! This spirit is vicious and will stop at nothing to rule and reign. She is cunning and persistent, and since she is rarely challenged, she will come at you with full force! It is vital to pray constantly for covering and protection from the Lord. It is most important to pray without ceasing!

The Baal's and Ashtoreth

In the original vision of the Hierarchy, The Lord spoke to my spirit saying, "There are five Baal's who rule under Ahab, Jezebel and Leviathan." I wrote them on a poster board and he began to give me their characteristics. The place I live in has the largest county in our state. There are so many sub communities with names, I couldn't begin to figure out in my natural mind which ones had the ruling Baal's, besides the obvious, the main town. God gave me the five communities and I charted them.

I was telling one of our members the next day, and he confirmed there were five districts in our town. When he named them, they were the five I had charted. A short time later, we would get another confirmation. Stopping at a gas station, my friend pointed to a large sign with a map of our county, we walked across the parking lot and saw the five districts on the map with circles drawn around them. I began to ask God the names of each Baal. It took several days and I had all but one. My friend and I decided to drive into the town one day, and as soon as we hit the little city limit, I received its name. It was Baal Baasha.

This one on my chart only had three characteristics, religion, pride and legalism. I remember distinctly how it felt too me. It was the most disgusting, gross, repulsive feeling I have ever felt! I exclaimed to my friend that it felt more unclean than the town that had the spirits of occultism and witchcraft. This really opened my eyes to how religious pride looks to God. I could not wait to get out of that town! I exclaimed

' I believe we could go sit in a brothel and it would feel cleaner than this place! (By now you must be thinking I am a freak, that only sees and feels evil! I assure I do not, the gift of discernment works both ways, you see and sense anointing and good as well. But even then, it is only as the Lord sees fit. I am very much a regular person, working out my salvation daily, just like everyone else.)

The Hebrew word for Baal is translated to mean "master' or "lord". They are much lower in rank than the main three principalities. I had written under them on my original chart their assignments. They rule political and government leaders and systems. They receive their power from the chosen people who commit spiritual adultery against God.

In fact my group, this very week, have had four dreams, from four different people and the recurring theme in each one was about adultery! We were in the middle of the battle and God was showing us that we were still fornicating with these spirits. He was pushing us, prodding us and causing us to continue cleansing ourselves. He was showing us we were being quite stubborn. We decided to start having more prayer meetings. That would be our social life. He would need to be our continual focus. My dream consisted of this; a man would come to my door and ask me to go on a date with them, I said, no and shut the door. A woman was in the background and she had the cold seductive eyes of Jezebel, and I knew somehow she was sending them. A second man came to my door and asked me to go on a date with him. I said no and shut the door. The third time a red Camaro pulled up in front of me and again, I was asked to go on a date, this time I said, I am married, leave me alone! And poof, I woke up. This was indicative to me that Jezebel was trying to seduce me to commit adultery, spiritual adultery. I had to refute her three times.

This is what happened to the great King Solomon. In the beginning of his life, he was known for his wisdom and devotion to the one true God. It was through him that the first temple was built. However he had inherited his father's lust. Solomon was a man of unbridled lust. The Bible tells us that he had seven hundred wives and three hundred concubines. They would eventually lead to his undoing, and the kingdom would be divided into twelve pieces. God would remove ten of the twelve tribes of Israel from the Israelites because of Solomon's sin." **And the Lord was angry with Solomon, because his heart had turned away from the Lord, the God of Israel, who had appeared to him twice and commanded him concerning this thing that he should not go after other gods. But he did not keep what the Lord commanded. Therefore the Lord said to Solomon, 'Since this has been your practice and you have not kept my covenant and my statutes that I have commanded you, I will surely tear the kingdom from you and will give it to your servant. Yet for the sake of your father David, I will not do it in your days, but I will tear it out of the hand of your son. However, I will not tear away the entire kingdom, but I will give one tribe to your son, for the sake of David my servant and for the sake of Jerusalem that I have chosen. "1 Kings 11:30-34.**

He allowed his wives to build groves and altars to the goddess Ashtoreth and to serve the Baal's. He even began to honor them as well. The most wise man on the planet fell for the trap Satan had planted! I believe at the end of his life, we see in Ecclesiastes that he is moaning and groaning. He has seen that all his accomplishments, woman, and wealth were all vanity, and brought him no pleasure. He had lost his joy in the Lord. Hear his words in Ecclesiastes 1 " **For in much wisdom is much grief and he that increases in knowledge increases in sorrow" Vs. 18**

Ashtoreth has many names- the goddess of war and fertility is also called Ishtar, the Queen of Heaven, Artemis and Diana. She has many more names, but she is a demonic spirit that serves Jezebel. In her temples were cult prostitution, it is said that beside her temples were mass graves of infants bones. While the people prayed to her for fertility and good luck in war, she required them to pay heavy sacrifices. If we serve her master today, we will also sacrifice our natural and spiritual children to the mass graves of spiritual death. I believe she is the reason for many miscarriages today. Because of her knowledge of war, it is she who attacks God's people so viciously.

I had an encounter with this spirit a few years ago. I had been praying over someone in our home. Later as I was getting ready for bed, I saw a demon pacing around my living room as if it was angry, it looked right at me and I suddenly knew it's name: Artemis. It wasn't until this writing that I realized Artemis is just another name for Ashtoreth. It looked anything but feminine. It had a blackened muscular body and its head looked like a gargoyle and its eyes were solid red, like a fiery coal. It exuded hatred of me through its eyes. I told my husband, shut the door and went to bed. I told him not to worry, as it seemed it couldn't get very close to us. He rebuked it, but it would come back a few more times. One night I said, "Lord, I am tired of this thing walking around in my house, please make it leave." I never saw it again after that.

Some scholars believe it is the spirit that Catholics pray to when they pray to Mary, because she is also called the Queen of Heaven. I do not know if that is whom they pray to, but I do suspect it is a demon. Jesus instructed us in Luke chapter 11, to pray to the Father in his name. We should not send prayers to saints, virgins or anyone else, because if we do, we are praying to demons. When Muslims pray to Allah and Mohammed they are praying to Moloch and the moon God. You can see it in their fruit. Moloch required child sacrifice. The Muslims teach their sons and daughters to be martyrs. Telling them and believing that if they die as martyrs, they will receive virgins in paradise, and that their whole families will be saved.

In this way the fruit of Moloch is easy to see. In war they often use women and children as shields. My son served in the war in Afghanistan. They were taught not to trust anyone, even the children. Historians believe that when Abraham was called by God and told to leave his people behind, that they were worshippers of the 'Moon God'. We know that the Arabs come from Abraham through Ishmael. The symbol for Islam is of a crescent moon and a star. There is also rampant sodomy in Afghanistan. Since they have viewed women as dogs for so many centuries, this is now the fruit. Ask any soldier about this, it is common knowledge. Even the ones we trained stayed in separate camps, I am told and at night would "smoke hash and have sex with one another."

The Bible forbids us in several passages about worshipping the moon, the sun and the stars. Here is one example. **" And he did away with the idolatrous priests whom the kings of Judah had appointed to burn incense to Baal, to the sun and to the moon and to the constellations and to all the host of heaven. " 2 Kings 23:5.**

I am pleased to hear of Muslims being converted all over the world, though it often cost them their lives. Many report that Jesus himself appears to them in dreams and visions. This is an indication of the end-time harvest. Only our Lord could do such things. Revelation Chapter eleven also speaks of the two witnesses sent by God to prophesy a ' thousand two hundred and three score days', they will do miracles and signs and wonders will follow them. This will be for the sons of Ishmael and Isaac. They will eventually be killed, and will lie in the streets for all to see for three days. The spirit will enter them again and they will rise and return to God. Upon their death, it says, the kingdoms will rejoice because the two prophets "tormented those who dwelt on earth." After their death, will be a great earthquake, and many will die. The Bible says that a "remnant " will be afraid and give glory to God.

Pray for peoples around the world to be open to the Holy Spirit. I can only imagine how it must feel to be under that type of vexation. I thank God every day that I was born in America, where we have freedom of religion. However, that privilege can be taken away from us. It is important to know and study your Bible. There may come a day when those will be taken away. We will be easily swayed if we do not carry the truth in our hearts. We will be deceived if we do not walk in spirit and truth. We must get free, and be able to hear Gods voice clearly, preparing for perilous times. Our rights are diminishing right now. Things are shifting and time seems to be speeding up. We must study to be approved." **These shall make war with the lamb, and the lamb shall overcome them: for he is KING of KINGS and LORD of LORDS: and they that are with him are called, and chosen and Faithful" Revelation 17:14**

Chapter Ten: The Visions of Ezekiel and the Temple of God

I am going to start this chapter based on another, very recent dream; my husband, I and my friend and elder in the ministry were sitting in a church on a pew. We were facing forward and a bunch of people were facing us, also sitting in pews. We were not lifted up higher than anyone, and we were not on a stage. They all seemed to be having a great discussion, and we were sitting quietly. I could not make out what they were saying. Suddenly a man looked straight at me and said," So you are saying, there are demons out there?" and he pointed out side. I said "Yes, that is what I am saying." Then he said," And you are saying there are demons in here?" I said, yes, that is what I am saying." Then he got animated and said "There can be no demons in here, this is Gods House!" To which I replied, "I say to you there are demons out there, there are demons in here, and there are demons in you." At that point I woke up.

I pondered it for a while. I knew it meant something. I am not one that has so many dreams in a row. But I have had enough to know which are from God and which are not. As I thought about this, the Holy Spirit kept whispering to my mind, "Study Ezekiel." So I did.

While Jeremiah lived to witness many of his prophecies be fulfilled, Ezekiel did not. He was a Priest and an exile, a captive of the Babylonians when he wrote that he saw ' visions of God.' Like Jeremiah, God told him he would have to harden himself to be able to speak to His people, for they were rebellious and stiff hearted. He told him they would most likely not hear him, but it would be a testimony against them, that there had been a prophet among them (Every time there has been a prophetic word or a prophet of God sent to you and you refuse it, it will be used as a testimony against you on judgment day. We will not be able to say, "Lord, I did not know, you did not tell me"). This is what Ezekiel had to speak. He was handed a book and he described its contents were" lamentations, mourning, and woe". He instructed him to eat it and go and speak to the people in covenant with God, the house of Israel. When he ate the book it was sweet but then turned bitter in his belly. This wasn't going to be a fun project for Ezekiel, and he knew it.

He had him demonstrate and do some very strange things, to show the people physically what their true spiritual condition was. (See Ezekiel chapter 1-7) Starting in chapter 8, he describes a being or an angel that took him by ' the lock of his hair' and lifted him up between earth and heaven. He was seeing into the spirit realm. " **And he put forth the form of an hand, and took me by a lock of mine head; and the spirit lifted me up between the earth hand heaven, and brought me in the visions of God to Jerusalem, to the door of the inner gate that looks toward the north; where was the seat of the image of jealousy, which provokes to jealousy. And behold the glory of the God of Israel was there, according to the vision that I saw in plain. Then he said unto me, son of man, lift up thine eyes now the way toward the north. So I lifted up my eyes the way toward the north, and behold northward at the gate of the altar this image of jealousy in the entry. He said furthermore unto me, Son of man, do you see what they do? Even the great abominations that the**

house of Israel do here, that I should go far off from my sanctuary? But turn thee yet again, and thou shall see greater abominations. And he brought me to the court; and when I looked, behold a hole in the wall. Then he said son of man, dig now in the wall: and I had digged in the wall, behold a door. And he said unto me, Go in, and behold the wicked abominations that they do here. So I went and saw; and behold every form of creeping things, and abominable beasts, and all the idols of the house of Israel, portrayed upon the wall round about." Ezekiel 8:3-10

History tells us that the temple of Jerusalem had already been destroyed. So what temple and sanctuary was he seeing? There are differing opinions on this subject, however Paul writes in the New Testament, " **Know ye not that ye are the temple of God, and that the spirit of God dwells in you?" 1 Corinthians 3:16.**

The context of this chapter is about fornicating with other gods. Read it closely, in verse 9 he states, you are God's husbandry, ye are God's building, and that the foundation of our faith is through Jesus Christ. We are called to be the bride of Christ. We have a marriage covenant, so to speak with Him. **1 Thessalonians 4 " For this is the will of God, even your sanctification that ye should abstain from fornication: that every one of you should know how to possess his vessel in sanctification and honor. Not in the lust of concupiscence, (desire, craving, desire for what is forbidden, lust), even as the Gentiles which know not God") VS 3-4.** He was speaking to the believers, the church. It is no wonder that God had Ezekiel use sexual symbolism in many of his prophecies. He showed him that by going after other gods, they were committing adultery, defiling the temple and that it was and is an abomination that he will not overlook. We know well Ezekiel's prophecies about the valley of dead dry bones. We know he speaks of Gog and Magog. Ezekiel had vision for the future and the end times. I believe he was seeing the condition of our temples as well.

He speaks of a gate in chapter 44,"**Then he brought me back the way of the gate of the outward sanctuary which looks toward the east; and it was shut. Then said the Lord unto me; this gate shall be shut, it shall not be opened, and no man shall enter in by it; because the LORD, the God of Israel, hath entered in by it, therefore it shall be shut. It is for the prince; the prince, he shall sit in it to eat bread before the Lord; he shall enter by the way of the porch of that gate, and shall go out by the way of the same." vs.1-3.** This makes me think of Jesus. **"I am the WAY the TRUTH and the LIFE: no man comes unto the Father, but by me."John 14:6 He also said " Enter ye at the straight gate: for wide is the gate, and broad is the way, that leads to destruction, and many there be which go there: Because strait is the gate, and narrow is the way, which leads to life, and few there be that find it' Matthew 7:13-14. When** I read this, I understand that a good many people, who believe that they will find Jesus but continue to live a sloppy, lukewarm life, may be deceived. I know about His grace and mercy, but we must accept all parts of God and his nature. Not just the parts we like.

How can I have devils? I have the Holy Spirit!

For many years, I cast out demons, not even knowing where they came from. The Jewish people understood demons. They never questioned their existence, the way we do today. They only questioned Jesus' ability to make them obey him. Modern technology has given us access to the Internet. Through it I stumbled upon the book of Enoch. It always bugged me that the book of Jude referenced him as a prophet. And other scriptures like 2 Peter chapter 2 always puzzled me. I decided to 'try the spirits" and read the first book of Enoch. I will not quote from it now, but it describes exactly where demons came from. They are the spirits of the giants referenced in Genesis that were born from Angels mating with women and bore them children. They were referred to as giants that devoured all of man's food and began to eat human flesh. The earth could not sustain them, Thus ushering in the flood that spared only Noah, his offspring and the animals. According to Enoch, God told them that since the offspring were not born of heaven that they would be bound here on earth, and would be called evil spirits. He repeatedly states that there function would be to vex, torment and attack the elect, because of this punishment. The fallen angels too are bound here. These spirits are trapped in earth's atmosphere. The angels were created for the heavens. They had whole galaxies to roam in. But because of their great sin and disobedience, they are cursed to this place. Over time they have become deformed and distorted, just as they have distorted our planet. There is no light in them and they cannot approach the light of God anymore.

I believe the higher principalities we battle are the angels that committed these acts that 'altered' the world. It explains why they despise us so much. Because God would not pardon them, they are trapped here as disembodied spirits. Enoch states that the Lord said because they were not born of heaven, they could not enter heaven. And the angels, who sinned with human women, were bound on earth for their disobedience. God refused to pardon their sin. There hatred for us is all they have left.

The only way to act out there evil nature is through us. (See Matthew 12:43 and Luke 11:24) If it were not for Jesus, we would be their prey, with no power to thwart them. This is a very important thing that Jesus died to give us, and it breaks my heart that he gets very little credit for it in today's church. Just as it was in the time our Lord walked the earth, deliverance, healing and salvation are for the people in covenant. He made one exception in Matthew 15:26-28. It was because of the gentile woman's great faith that he answered her plea for her daughter to be cleansed from the demon. I have never successfully cast a devil out of an unrepentant, unbeliever. It is pointless to even try. Here is the scripture that most like to challenge the need for deliverance with. **"But he was wounded for our transgressions; he was bruised for our iniquities: the chastisement of our peace was upon Him, and with His stripes we are healed." Isaiah 53:5**

People argue that there is no need for Christians to battle the enemy. They are sadly mistaken. Read the rest of the Bible. We are not in the dispensation they believe we are in. Until Christ returns we must put on our armor and battle for the kingdom of God. That is the power of the name and authority of Jesus Christ. That is the power that should rest in you and me.

When you are sick, do you pray for healing? Yes. If we did not need to appropriate the work of the cross, and do the works of Jesus ourselves, we would never be sick or have demons in our flesh." **Verily, verily, I say unto you, He that believeth on me, the works that I do shall he do also; and greater works than these shall he do; because I go to the Father." John 14:12.**

Are we seeing 'greater works'? Examine HIS works, all of them, and do them. Fast, pray, rebuke the devil, teach, heal, prophesy, cast out demons, and command the weather as according to your gifts. Do these things and we will see mighty revival. We must do the works while we still can!

We cannot put God in a doctrinal box and expect Him to stay there. The Church does not fear the Lord nor effectively battle the devil. We have been deceived greatly by thinking Satan cannot touch us. Where there is darkness and sin, there we will find the devil and his demons. And if we are truly honest with ourselves, we all have darkness and sin in us. Why are there so many diseases? Why are so many children perishing from cancer and other diseases today? Could it be because we are unwilling to battle the devil for them? **"And Jesus rebuked the devil, and he departed out of him, and the child was cured from that very hour" Matthew 17:18**

Satan has effectively wiped out one the main principals of the doctrine of Jesus Christ. And the Church has not only allowed it, they have promoted it! Sometimes I wonder to myself, "do people read the same Bible that I read?' Am I that far off the beam? I would rather my life and my belief systems reflect the words in the scripture, than the doctrines of men!' **He that saith he abides in HIM ought himself also to walk, even as he walked" 1 John 2:6. In** other words, we are to be doing the things our Lord did. That is what He sacrificed to give us, salvation and the power of the Holy Ghost. **"Behold, I give you power to tread on serpents and scorpions, and over all the power of the enemy: and nothing shall by any means hurt you." Luke 10:19**

The book of Ezekiel uses sexual references continually throughout. He uses the word whoredoms nineteen times, the term harlot nine times, and the term abominations thirty three times. In chapter 16, The Lord describes how he feels about their adultery, or their 'cheating' on Him. **"Son of man causes Jerusalem to know her abominations."**

He then describes how they had been born in rejection and spiritual filthiness, and he had great pity on them. He then caused them to multiply and grow. He decked them with ornaments of beauty and **'spread my skirt over thee, and covered thy nakedness: yea, I swore unto thee, and entered into a covenant with thee ,thus saith The Lord GOD, and thou became mine' vs. 3-8**. He describes how he anointed them and prospered them and made them beautiful. The affirmation and blessing of the Lord was not enough for them, they began to desire the heathen and their approval over God's. They began to pollute themselves by worshipping idols.

They had forgotten God. In verse 38 God says **"And I will judge thee, as a woman that breaks wedlock and shed blood are judged; and I will give thee blood in fury and jealousy."**

The modern Church is no different! Our idols are our downfall. We lust for power, money, wealth and constant entertainment. Our homes are full of strife, false peace and rebellion. We are living in a delusion, and deception is a way of life. We say he is our God, but refuse Him when he convicts of us sin. When his fire falls upon us to purge us, we blame it on the devil, or someone else. We have a deaf and dumb spirit. We refuse to hear or speak godly correction. Our flesh rules us. Our spirit man is left hungry and vulnerable.

Americans and many other peoples have no idea what true persecution feels like. We believe that if anyone disagrees with us, that is persecution. We are unwilling to allow God to de-bunk our spiritual doctrines that are wrong. We have been taught by men, not God. Many will never spend time in prayer and the study of God's word. We want to be fed all of our lives, like babies on the breast" **For when for the time ye ought to be teachers, ye have need that one teach you again which be the first principles of the oracles of God; and are become such as have need of milk, and not of strong meat " Hebrews 5**. We stand on our pride and forsake humility. Our unbelief keeps us in bondage." **And He (Jesus) did not many mighty works there because of their unbelief". Matthew 13:58**

We must forsake our false doctrines, and false repentance to press into the strong meat from God's table. Perilous times are upon us; the return of our Savior is imminent. The day is coming when we will have to stand behind the things we are serving; every hidden thing will be revealed. He is coming for a spotless bride. He is coming for those who are humble, correctable, and pure of heart. Our flesh will never stop sinning, so we have to allow the Holy Spirit to shine his light upon us, that we may repent and change, and bear good fruit. Jesus said a good tree would bear good fruit; a corrupt tree will bear corrupt fruit. Good fruit is true humility, obedience and loyalty to the God we serve. The early church understood this. Many of them lost their lives for the kingdom of God. They were loyal.

The book of Revelation says that true believers would overcome (the enemy) by the blood of the lamb, and they would not love their lives but would die for the great cause of Christ. We do not see a picture of a pampered spoiled church. We see a faithful, militant church in the pages of Revelation. They were Militant in prayers and war against Satan and his kingdom. They were faithful to God until the bitter end. That is the true church. The feel good all the time prosperity teachers are not preparing the children of God for what lies ahead. They prepare you for failure. They prepare you for hell.

From beginning and until the end, we will be plagued with false prophets. They are boldly taking over the pulpits. Those that are true are so smitten and afflicted, they feel unworthy and afraid to speak truth! I know every time I have had to see into the spirit realm, it leaves me feeling like a worm, like my righteousness is as filthy rags. I see that no matter how hard I try, I cannot stop sinning! God has rebuked me for this. He has 'put a fire in my belly' to speak the truth, Knowing all the while that I am not worthy. It is HIS righteousness that I am to promote anyways, not my own. He looks at our hearts and our desire to obey him. He does the work; we just have to be willing. When he requires us to get clean, it is for our benefit and because he loves us much. Even while being purged we can rest in his mercy. We must put away our timidity and our inability to be persecuted and stand up!

Ezekiel 13 says it best and gives us an understanding of what following and teaching the false looks like to God "**Thus saith the Lord GOD; Woe unto the foolish prophets, that follow their <u>own</u> spirit, and have seen nothing! O Israel, thy prophets are like the foxes in the deserts. Ye have not gone up into the gaps, neither made up the hedge for the house of Israel to <u>stand in battle in the day of the LORD.</u> They have seen vanity and lying divination, saying, The Lord saith: and the LORD hath not sent them: and they have made others to <u>hope</u> that they would confirm the word. Have ye not seen a vain (worthless, empty) vision, and have ye not spoken a lying divination, whereas ye say, The LORD saith it; albeit I have not spoken. Therefore thus saith The LORD GOD; because ye have spoken vanity, and seen lies, therefore, behold, I am against you, saith the LORD GOD. And my hand shall be upon the prophets that see vanity, and that divine lies: they shall not be in the assembly of my people, neither shall they be written in the writing of the house of Israel, neither shall they enter into the land of Israel; and ye shall know that I am the LORD GOD. Because even though they have seduced my people, saying, Peace; and (when) there is no peace; and one built up a wall, and, lo, others daubed it with untempered (foolish) mortar: Say unto them which daub it with untempered mortar, that it shall fall: there shall be no overflowing shower; and yea, O great hailstones, shall fall; and a stormy wind shall rend it. Lo, when the wall is fallen, shall it not be said unto you, Where is the daubing (coating) wherewith you daubed it?" Ezekiel 13:3-12.**

You might be saying sister, what does this mean? I tell you that it means that when we listen to the false and follow them, it is because we are following after the lusts of man's hearts and not God's. It means the walls we have built against the truth are foolishness in the eyes of God. It will not stand nor protect you from the enemy. The Holy Spirit cannot rain down on us, so therefore a storm and hailstones will destroy us. This is why it is vital that each individual build a relationship with God. Let him teach you his voice, learn His word. Believe Him, for He never lies. Don't let the fate of your soul be left up to man's understanding. Pray and ask God for wisdom. Study Proverbs. The Bible says wisdom cries out in the streets, looking for someone to hear and listen and obey!

I pray right now that you receive the gift of Godly wisdom! I pray that you would surround yourself with people who follow the Lord and speak wisdom to you. I pray for you that you receive understanding. I pray for you to be bold in The WORD OF GOD! I bind the enemy and the false from your mind, in the mighty name of JESUS!

Chapter Eleven: The Spirit of Jehu

Not long after the fast, we had been having a prayer meeting in our home. After everyone left, the Lord spoke to my spirit. He instructed me to anoint my husband with oil. I went to the kitchen and grabbed a bottle of olive oil. As I began praying, I spoke, "I do anoint and speak to you that you will rise up and walk in the spirit of Jehu." He sat there, and I could tell the Lord was moving on him. I could see in his face that something wonderful was happening between him and the Lord. I left him alone, and went into another room. He stayed in prayer awhile longer. When he came to bed that night, I saw and sensed he was afraid and conflicted. I sensed he felt unworthy. I left it alone for many weeks. I needed God to prove this word to him, not me.

Until that point I hadn't thought much about Jehu. I decided to study up on him and was astonished that his personality was exactly like that of my husband! Jehu was a man with a black and white personality, so is my husband. I am a person that sees the colors and shades. I tend to need many confirmations from God before I act. I tend to long suffer and allow people to mistreat me, and the flock, ever hoping they will see the light of God and change. My husband was not this way. If God showed him something was right, it was right. End of discussion. He is a businessman with the utmost integrity, but if he had to fire someone for slacking or not doing his or her job, he did it. Saying," they don't care about their job, why should I let them ruin others who do? They have fired themselves and I have to be the person who tells them." It seems Jehu was the same.

God had spoken to the prophet Elijah and told him to anoint Jehu the son of Nimshi to be king over Israel, and to anoint Elisha to be the prophet to take his place. Elijah had pled with God to let him be released after his dealings with Ahab and Jezebel. The Bible says that Elijah was taken into heaven by a chariot of fire, and he went up to heaven in a whirlwind (tornado). (2 Kings Chapter 2) Elijah never tasted physical death. He simply was taken up.

" And Elisha the prophet called one of the prophets, and said to him, gird up thy loins, and take this box of oil in thine hand, and go to Ramothgilead: And when you come there, look out there Jehu the son of Jehoshaphat the son of Nimshi, and go in and make him arise up from among his brethren, and carry him to an inner chamber; then take the box of oil, and pour it thus on his head, and say, Thus saith the Lord, I have anointed thee king over Israel." 2 Kings 9:1-3 Elisha did that and gave him specific instructions, Jehu was to "smite the house of Ahab" to avenge the blood of the slain prophets and servants of God. Then he was told Jezebel's fate as well. Jehu basically said, is this true? Then he went forth and did exactly as the Lord had instructed.

It is told that when Jehu went for Jezebel, she sent spies to ask him why he was there, and was he coming to make peace. He didn't answer them at first, saying, turn thee behind me. The spy reported that this Jehu" driveth furiously". In other words, he was driven to obey and accomplish God's commandments concerning Ahab's descendants, Jezebel, and the kingdom of Israel. Where Elijah had hidden in a cave, Jehu seemed to care less about her or her status as a vicious witch!

Jezebel then sends her son, Joram out to meet him saying, is it peace, Jehu? I love his answer! He replied, matter of factly, **"What peace, as long as the whoredoms of thy mother Jezebel and her witchcrafts are so many?' 2 Kings 9:22.** He was exactly right. There would be and can be no peace as long as we placate Jezebel. Her witchcrafts are just too much. The Bible says that Jehu entered Jezebel's gate. She had painted her face and fixed her hair, in an attempt to seduce him. **She looked out her window and said, " Is it peace, you (son of) Zimri, murderer of your master? And he (Jehu) lifted up his face to the window and said who is on my side? Who? Two or three eunuchs looked out at him. He said, throw her down. So they threw her down. And some of her blood splattered on the wall and on the horses, and they trampled on her.' Verse 31-33.**

Spirits of Jezebel, Ahab and Leviathan hate peoples with the Jehu anointing! Their fierceness, cunning, and manipulating ways will not sway these types. He went on and obeyed the Lord, and slew all of Ahab's descendants. Next he kills all the prophets of Baal. 2 Kings Chapter 10 says that, Jehu completely wiped out Baal worship from Israel. He turned the house of Baal into a latrine! The only problem he had was in the end; he walked in the curse of Solomon's successor.

The sins of Jeroboam were idol worship as well. His sin was in erecting golden calves to keep the people from going to Solomon's temple. It was a political move to keep power. The Lord rebuked Jehu, but promised his sons would sit on the throne of Israel for four generations, because he had obeyed him concerning the house of Ahab.

This story shows that at all times we must walk in the ways of the Lord and with God. When we walk in our on understanding, we fail. As deliverance ministers, some of the things we see and do, the battle must not take precedence over whom we battle for. We can minister deliverance to the masses, and still lose our own souls. We cannot have one ounce of prideful ambition in us to accomplish this work. We cannot walk in rebellion, and hear his voice. I made that mistake once, and I suffered, my family suffered, and I carry the burden of it to this day.

My story of rebellion against God:

After the second dealings with Leviathan, Ahab and Jezebel, I sinned greatly against God. Unlike the first time when I was persecuted and hurt so deeply, instead of praying, releasing and forgiving, I became bitter and angry. I became bitter at God.

I remember saying to Him, God, I love you but I HATE your people! This gift you have given me is a curse! I want nothing more to do with it. I had always been blessed with the ability to see, and to hear the Lord clearly. I could not understand why everyone else couldn't. My first spiritual dream came to me as a new Christian. I dreamt I was standing on a rock, on it were the words **Colossians 2:10 "Ye are complete in him who is head of all principality and power".**

Even in the beginning of my relationship with the Lord, He was showing me I would be gifted in deliverance. That's how I learned the Bible. I would ask the Lord a question and he would respond instantly saying, Daughter, read Luke 11 etc.... I often joked that the Lord spoke to me in the language of the King James. Not long after I said these words to God, it was as if a light bulb went off. When I tried to pray, all I heard was silence. This went on for at least a year.

In that year, Satan would have his way with me. I became severely depressed, very rebellious. My youngest child was leaving for college, my oldest was joining the army to fight the Taliban, and I could not hear God to save my life. I started trying to fill that hole with the world. I worked and picked up some bad habits and I eventually left my beloved husband. God was having none of that. My Jehu husband stayed faithful to me. He describes it as the most painful time in his life, yet it drew him to the Lord, more than ever. I would ask for divorce, and he would say,' What God has joined, let no man separate.' He would not budge. I know that while I was away, he spent long hours in prayer and tears, pleading for our marriage and for my health. He lost so much weight, I barely recognized him when I would see him.

I had begun to have seizures. I knew it was demonic, but I had no power to stop it. My prayers went no higher than my ceiling, so it felt. I came back home, and my husband cared for me. I had days where I would go catatonic. Frozen, unable to speak or even feed myself. He would read the Bible to me and pray. It seemed everyone had abandoned me, except him. One night in a state of despair, I could not take the emotional pain anymore. I swallowed a handful of Valium and Advil. As I lay down to die, I heard a whisper in my spirit, 'this is not my plan for you, but Satan's. Do you not fear hell?" I managed to alert my husband, all I could do was point to the empty pill bottle, but he knew what I had done. He took me to the emergency room.

It would take many more months before I could hear God's voice again. When I did, he said to me. "You have taken me lightly; you have taken my voice for granted. You must never do that again." Any time I feel rejected by man, I know to look back on that experience. Anytime we feel tempted to walk away from our call, we both know we cannot.

The beauty of the relationship we have with the Lord, trumps everything at the end of the day. I understand that peoples sometimes do things, and cannot hear God for themselves. I know that demonic powers speak to them, and I know that we have to have mercy and do something about it. I learned through this not to take God for granted, and I am learning to love His people. Many in my own family have mocked, persecuted and reviled me. Though it hurts, I know I cannot expect to get affirmation from man. In His great mercy, God has put loyal people in my life, who appreciate and support the work we do, helping in any way they can. But they are few and far between in the kingdom. Most people are in it for what they can get for themselves.

We all have to come to the place where we are willing to obey God, even if we are left totally alone and abandoned by men. I say this to warn you. To defeat the enemy of our souls, you will receive opposition. You have to get used to persecution. You have to forgive and pray for your enemies. It is spiritual law put in place to protect YOU. It is also an act of love. Our merciful savior taught us this on the cross. As he was being crucified he spoke these words **"Father, forgive them; for they know not what they do" Luke 23:34.** This was not a show of false humility; it was a true petition to God for our forgiveness. His heart was for us until the bitter end, and still is today.

Chapter Twelve: Discernment, is it for me?

Over the years, many people would say to me, "I do not have the gift of discernment; therefore I cannot help what I do." I wanted to take this opportunity to talk about that mind set. Let us look at the Word of God regarding this topic." **Now concerning spiritual gifts, brethren, I would not have you ignorant...Now there are diversity of gifts, but the same Spirit. And there are differences of administrations, but the same Lord. And there are diversities of operations, but it is the same God, which worketh all in all. But the manifestation of the Spirit is given to every man to profit withal. For to one is given by the Spirit the word of wisdom; to another the word of knowledge by the same Spirit; to another faith by the same spirit; to another the gifts of healing by the same Spirit; To another the working of miracles; to another prophecy; to another discerning of spirits; to another divers kinds of tongues; to another the interpretation of tongues: But all these worketh that one and the selfsame Spirit, dividing to every man severally as he will." 1 Corinthian 12:1-11**

The gifts or manifestations are the parts that make up the whole of the power of the Holy Spirit. These are gifts given to men, for the brethren, to perform the things needed in the church according to HIS will. The root word for gift in this context is charisma meaning: A (divine) gratuity), i.e.. Deliverance (from danger or passion), (specially) a (spiritual endowment, i.e. (subjectively) religious qualification, or (objectively) miraculous faculty: (free) gift. The enemy and his kingdom have been very successful in stamping out and squashing these spiritual gifts, thereby stamping out the Holy Spirit. While all are seemingly dormant, I believe the gift of discerning of spirits is the most concealed gift of them all.

Then there is the measure of discernment that is given to all believers. Hebrews 5:14 tells us this **"Strong meat belongs to them that are of full age (mature Christians), even those who by reason of <u>use</u> have their senses exercised to discern both good and evil."** This reference describes a mature Christian who exercises his ability to discern good and evil. This discernment is for you, not the body. The gift of discernment is for the body of Christ and profits all.

The other form of discernment is for your own self, and benefits you. I will use the ministry of Jesus to show you the meaning. **"Behold, there was a woman which had a spirit of infirmity eighteen years, and was bowed together, and could in no wise lift herself up. And when Jesus saw her, he called her to him, and said unto her, Woman, thou art loosed from thine infirmity. And he laid his hands on her: and immediately she was made straight, and glorified God." Luke 13:11-13.** This woman clearly had a <u>spirit of infirmity.</u> When we get sick, and prayers for healing do not bring about deliverance, do we as leaders even consider the notion that it could be an unclean spirit causing the infirmity? What about anxiety and fear? The Bible calls them unclean spirits. Can you feel anxiety? Can you feel fear? If you can that is discernment. You must develop the habit of testing things with your Bible. The word of God is true, and everything it says has happened and will happen. It will not return void or undone. In 2010, researches estimated that 1 in 5 people in America take some form of medication for anxiety, including many children. Stress and anxiety are the driving forces behind heart disease, autoimmune disease and much more. The church is sending it's sheep to scientists and doctors, who rarely cure them, only manage their symptoms. We should measure our problems and seek counsel from the word of God. The scripture says, **"Be anxious for nothing; but in everything by prayer and fasting and supplication with thanksgiving let your requests be known to God. And the peace of God, which passes all understanding, shall keep your hearts and minds through Christ Jesus." Philippians 4:6**

I am not against doctors, I am thankful for them, but I see a different reality in the scripture than what I see in today's churches. If I had not understood that fear is a spiritual problem, I would be dead by now. If I had not cast out unclean spirits and spirits of infirmity, I would not be here today writing this. We can discern and feel anger, we can discern and feel unnatural fears, but we do not know what to do with these feelings. Everyone gets angry, but if you have a habitual problem with anger, it is very likely that it is a spiritual problem. The Bible says, "**Be ye angry, but sin not, let not the sun go down on your wrath." (Ephesians 4:26).**

If your anger is not measured in moments, but lasts for days, months even years, you could have an unclean spirit of bitterness and anger. Our discernment, if it is correct will always agree with the word of God. False discernment loves to see what is wrong with everyone else. You will know it is false by its critical nature. True discernment comes forth from a place of love; it comes to heal not wound.

In deliverance ministry, many times you have to fast and pray. You have to spend your time seeking God for a person or persons. It is an act of love, and is very hard work; it can be very taxing and time consuming.

If you do not love the person, and love the Lord, you will not want to be bothered with them. You will criticize, but will not lift a finger to help them get free. You are a Pharisee and a hypocrite.

The gift of discernment works like this, since you cannot feel what the person feels, and you cannot climb into their mind and hear their thoughts, you have to rely on the Holy Spirit to show you in prayer. The gift of discernment works closely with the gift of knowledge and healing. The deliverance minister will perceive thoughts, discern spirits and know things that the person has not told you. Many times you will see the wounds and traumas that brought in the spirits. In this way it is a gift of miracles as well. People who walk in this gift usually can rebuke storms and the like as well.

In the end times, this gift will be much needed. I found this in scripture that confirmed my instincts. **"And John saying, Master, we saw one casting out devils in thy name, and he does not follow us: and we forbade him, because he follows not us. But Jesus said, Forbid him not: for there is no man who shall do a miracle in my name that can lightly speak evil of me " Mark 9:39** I find this to be true. To do this type of work, you must understand who Jesus really is. You cannot take him lightly. You realize that you have a target on your back in the spirit realm, so you rely closely upon the Lord.

For me, each case is like putting together a puzzle. Each person is unique. It requires a type of focus that keeps you from doing fun things, like shopping and the like. When we have a case before us, I usually spend the majority of my time seeking God for that person. I have had to mature and find balance in my life. I have to rest in his mercy, until the answers come forth. He knows the right timing, He knows the persons heart, not I. I serve Him, not the other way around. I have had to battle the temptation to take on false burdens. Many times I would want the person to be free, when the persons themselves did not really desire to be.

This was revealed to me through prayer one night. I had been having body aches and fatigue. I asked the group to pray for me and the Holy Spirit revealed that I was entertaining a spirit of false burden. When I repented and cast it out, I began to feel better. It is something I keep a watch over. I guard my heart against it constantly. I have to trust the gifts and talents of my team members. One person cannot see everything. It is impossible to do this ministry alone and it takes great unity.

I prefer to work with small groups at a time. Your anointing may be different or greater than mine, and that's okay. Every deliverance minister has his or her own style and personalities. I prefer to do these things in private. I do not allow the sessions to be videotaped. It is a personal, humbling experience for the person getting prayer. I do not wish to put them on display. Others do it on camera, and Jesus obviously did it openly and in public. This is just my personal preference. I pray that God leads you in this area, and you begin to attack the enemy instead of always being attacked. I pray you will use your abilities for the kingdom of God. **"And the God of peace shall bruise Satan under your feet shortly. The grace of our Lord Jesus Christ be with you. Amen" Romans 16:20**

Chapter Thirteen: It's all about the Sheep

As I was receiving revelation and understanding of the false kingdom of Babylon, and the confusion it brought forth, my soul felt vexed with sorrow. I began to understand why many Christians looked like the walking wounded. I felt a new compassion for people that previously I had thought was rude or evil. I had felt that people were reaping what they deserved. I began to feel a love and mercy that I had not been able to feel before.

We see people all the time that simply cannot be civil, or kind. It always shocked me to see the lack of hospitality in and out of the church. Now I know, more than ever, that people are walking through this life carrying their wounds around, and it manifests in the physical as ugliness. I began to think, what must have happened to that person, for them to be so mean and un-loving?

Many times in ministry we would pray for healing of wounds. I sought the Lord, wondering if this was scriptural. Was wounds and traumas the cause of so many problems and tendencies to sin? I found the answer in Isaiah chapter one, **"Ah sinful nation, a people laden with iniquity, a seed of evil doers, children that are corrupters: they have forsaken the Lord, they have provoked the Holy One of Israel unto anger, they are gone away backward. Why should you be stricken and punished anymore? You will revolt more and more. The whole head is sick, and the whole heart is faint. From the sole of the foot even to the head there is no soundness or health- but wounds and bruises and fresh and bleeding stripes; they have not been pressed out and closed up or bound up or softened with oil (no one has troubled to seek a remedy) Verse 4** In other words generation after generation has walked in woundedness, passing the tendencies of rejection, fear and anger on to their children. When we have been wounded, we tend to act out in those wounds and hurt others. We tend to model to our children the images of sin and not the image of the Lord.

Many men that have come through our ministry doors will confess that they took on pride and drivenness to succeed because their parents told them they would never amount to anything. They were expected to fail which caused them to strive in the flesh to be somebody. Others give over to the idea that they are worthless, and walk in that direction, the path of failure. Many women come to us with histories of molestation, abuse and traumas. They harden their hearts to men, and become paranoid and full of fear, always expecting to be hurt or rejected. Or they become overly submissive and fearful if they do not continually please their mate, they will be cast aside. This is why it is important to not walk in the sins of our mothers and fathers. It is important to break these generational curses or tendencies. The buck must stop somewhere. The generational sins brought in through woundedness have piled up for so many generations now, that we are fulfilling the end time scripture of a people of cold love.

The Bible says our wounds and bruises have not been tended to. Deliverance and healing of wounds is part of the gift of salvation. A close walk with God can and will purge you, bring them to the surface and heal you. The Lord desires to soften you with the oil of the Holy Spirit. Psychologists and therapists almost always want you to discuss and UN-bury your wounds. They teach you that you are to get in agreement with your wounds and be okay with them. I tell you that you that you have a savior that wants to deliver you and set you free. You can feel the pain, and relive the memories until the cows come home, but in the end you need supernatural healing. You need to understand your worth comes from God, and through Him, you are precious and special, wanted and needed. Don't become one with your past, become an overcomer of your past. Understand that it does not define who you are or who you can be. When you can do that, then you are truly free.

An encounter with Jesus

During a prayer meeting recently, I began to feel such anguish and pain; my prayers were coming out as groaning. I felt such agony I went and pressed my body against a door. In the door, there was an image of the cross. I asked the Lord what I was feeling, what was this burden? Suddenly the door disappeared and I saw the lap of Jesus, I laid my head in his lap for a brief second and the image was gone. I turned and shouted to my group," It is about the sheep; Jesus is grieving for the sheep!"

I realized while in the presence of Jesus, I was able to feel his grief and burden for the sheep. His love for us is so great! It is indescribable! I feel He is waiting for that final piece of the puzzle to fall into place so that He can return and restore. The Bible tells us that the Lord will return when "the time of the gentiles is full." Jesus said that only the father knows when that will take place. I feel he is yearning, and grieving and ready to redeem us from this cursed place. We know in that day, Satan will be bound for one thousand years. We will experience a world ruled and dominated by God. We will experience paradise. The Bible also tells us that the believers will rule and reign with Christ on earth. He is purging us now for that day. I can't help but think that the least in the kingdom will receive the greatest honor. **"For he that is least among you all, the same shall be great." Luke 9:48**

I want to stand in the gap for you right now. I want to repent and apologize to you for every, pastor, mother, father or authority figure that did not love, protect and cover you. I want to tell you that it wasn't and isn't your fault. I ask you to forgive them and me. I want to speak a word to you of encouragement. You are much loved by God. He cares about you so deeply, no man can understand it. He feels your pain and he wants to heal you and anoint you. Will you let him? Whatever mountain is standing in your way and keeping you from feeling the love of God, I say to it be thou removed; I cast it into the sea, in Jesus name.

"But whoso shall offend one of these little ones which believe in me, it were better for him that a millstone were hanged about his neck, and that he were drowned in the depth of the sea. "Matthew 18:6

Chapter Fourteen: The Battle Plan

If you are now at the end of this book, this tells me you desire to do warfare against these spirits. I will give step-by-step instructions on how we did this in our group. The first spirit you must attack is Ahab. The person receiving prayer must repent:

Father, in the name of Jesus, I repent for entertaining or operating in the spirit of Ahab and any of his underlings. I ask you to forgive my forefathers, on both sides of my family tree and me and break all generational curses that have been placed upon my self and my offspring. I repent for all pride and haughtiness, and for ever speaking against your Holy Spirit.

I ask that you deliver me and set me free from the kingdom of Babylon. I bind the powers of Ahab in the heavenilies and I loose your warring angels on my behalf. I repent and sever all ties and chords between myself and all spirits of Jezebel and Leviathan.

Now you can begin to cast out the armor spirits of Ahab. You may sneeze, cough, sigh, moan, cry or even growl. Keep praying, this indication that they are leaving.

I bind all spirits from interfering with this deliverance. I am a servant to the most high God, The God of Israel, Jesus Christ of Nazareth and his Holy Spirit. I crush, destroy and smite the altars of all false gods. I tear down and destroy the groves of the enemy, in Jesus name.

(Now command each spirit to go in the name of Jesus Christ). In the name and authority of Jesus Christ of Nazareth, and through his precious blood I rebuke and cast out the spirits of:

Suffering
Destroyer
Death
Covetous authority
Stubbornness
Accusation
Frustration
Weakness
Selfishness
False love
Resistance
Aggression
Sorcery
Unrighteousness
Sullen
Betrayal
Mean/cruel
Gender confusion
Love of mammon
Trust in mammon
Distrust in God
Protecting evil
Death curse
Blood curse
Uncleanness
Fear
Defiling spirits
Failure

Doomed
Fornication with the eyes/mind
Mammon
Abbadon
Destruction
Craving distrust in God
Subjugation
Trickery
Bondage
Cunning
Slavery
Darkness
Murmuring and complaining
Disobedience
Submissive
Downcast spirits/depression
Belittling women
Worldliness
Defiling spirits
Hatred of women in authority
Inferiority
Rebellion of authority
Generational sexual sin
Disobedience
Condoning evil
Curse of not covering family/wife
Intimidation
Indecision

Passivity
Disdain
Evil thoughts
Untamed tongue
Greed
Railing doubt
Cursing
Abuse
Wickedness
Witchcraft
Rebellion
Control
Fear of responsibility
Worldliness
Selfish ambition
Generational subverted authority
Resistance
Bitterness towards women
Anger towards women
Control
Despising
Darkness
Carnal mindedness
Fantasy
Wrath
Daydream
Gods of the belly
Occupying mind spirits
High mindedness
Delusion
Succubus
Inordinate affection

Bullying
Hatred of women
Mistrust of women
Self will
Manipulation
Corruption
Baal
Occulted spirits
Vindictive
Antichrist spirit
Pride
Idolatry of wife/mother
Forked tongue
Pride of life
Ashtoreth
Pride of knowledge
Lilith
Know it all
Displeasure
Bragging
Simple minded
Double minded
Fear of losing control of wife
Insecurity
Addiction
Disobedience
Complacency
Passivity
Lust
Stubbornness
Accusation
Frustration
Racism

Now command all residual spirits to go in Jesus name. Now you can cast out Ahab himself. Keep rebuking him until he leaves!

Warfare can begin against Leviathan now.

In the name of Jesus Christ we bind and rebuke the spirit of Leviathan in the heaven lies. We break off all cords of sin and sever all ties with Ahab and Jezebel. We break and crush the scales of your pride, and smite the neck of Leviathan. The angel of the Lord rebukes you, Leviathan. We dry up your waters and cut off your strength by the power of Jesus. You were defeated at the cross. We are against your pride just as God opposes you. I ask the Healing oil of The Holy Spirit to bind up anoint and heal all wounds and traumas holding these spirits in place.

Lead the person in a repentance prayer as follows:

Father, I repent for entertaining, operating or tolerating Leviathan in my life. I ask you to forgive my forefathers on both sides, and break the generational curses off my life and my offspring. I repent for being haughty and unteachable or for ever speaking against your Holy Spirit. I humble myself before you mighty God, and ask for your great mercy in Jesus name.

Now command the spirits, by name to leave in the name of Jesus.

I command and break the crown of pride off the head and command all spirits to go and loose, in Jesus name.

Arrogance
Mischief
Haughtiness
Python
Abominations
Resistance
Spiritual slumber
Deaf and dumb
Doubt and unbelief
Fear of the Holy Spirit
Critical
Accusation
Cursing
Belittling

Selfism
Squid
Octopus spirits
Prideful look
Stubbornness
Rebellion
Calculating
Misogyny
Distorted view of women/men
Succubus/incubus
Unholy desires
Craving
Feeling small
Inferiority

Distrust
Paranoia
Familiar spirits
Fear of losing control
Suffering
Vexation
Serpent
Shame
Hiding
Guile
Adultery
Fornication
Idolatry of self
Witchcraft
Curse of warring against God's chosen
Hard hearted
Torture
Torment
Orion
Solaris
Dictatorship
Opposition
Smiting Gods anointed
Artemis
Ishtar
Unyielding
Unrepentance
Rebuttal
Children of pride
Haughty neck
Tolerating Jezebel
Hatred
Viciousness
Fierce
Cruel
Sarepis
Simplemindedness
Memory loss
Ashtoreth
Anger
Rage
Wrath
Gods of the belly
Divisions
Needing to be right (uncorrectable)
Fist of wickedness
Froward mouth
Pride of knowledge
Pride of looks
False spirits
False worship
Mockery
Backbiting
False humility
False praise
False vision
Complaining/murmurring
Strife
Envy
Jealousy
Moloch
Subverted authority
Sorcery
Familiar spirits
Extreme anger and rage
Mockery
Spiritual laziness
Spiritual idolatry
Spiritual adultery
Legion

Now command all residual spirits that answer to Leviathan to leave and rebuke the spirit of Leviathan. He is stubborn, but persists. Play worship music and read warfare scriptures. Resist him until he leaves!

Now it is time to uproot Jezebel. (These things should not be done all at once. Allow time and space for repentance. The person praying and the persons receiving prayer will be exhausted. We only attempt two sessions at a time in our ministry)

I bind the spirit of Jezebel in the heaven lies and in the room. I sever your tentacles, Jezebel, and break your demonic influence. I break the cords of your covens and sever you from them. You will not receive strength from them any longer. We break your Baal's and tear down your groves. We call fire down from heaven to consume your idols, in Jesus name. I ask for the healing of all trauma and abuse that may have brought in and strengthened Jezebel. Lead the person in a repentance prayer as follows:

Father, in the name of Jesus, I repent for operating, entertaining or functioning in the spirit of Jezebel and Ashtoreth. I ask you to forgive my forefathers on both sides, and break the generational curse off my offspring and me. I ask you to consume these spirits by your purifying fire. I ask you raise a watch over my soul against these wicked demons. I serve and obey the one true God of Israel, Jesus Christ and his Holy Spirit; I appropriate the blood of Jesus over my life, amen.

Now command the following spirits to leave in the name of Jesus Christ:

Extreme anxiety
Sorcery
Slander
Lying
Gossiping
Back biting

Guile
Treachery
Shedding innocent blood
Abuse
Critical spirits
Anti-christ

Manipulation
Control
Evil thoughts
Baal
Abominations
Murder
Disdain for men
Rejection
Trickery
Raven
Deceit
Idolatry
Confusion
Babbling
Aggression
Accusation
False repentance
False vision
Usurping authority
Gold digger
Unnatural affection
Belligerent
Rebellion
Self pity
Sulking
Plotting
Scheming
Failure
Defeat
Infirmity
Curse of touching God's anointed
Queen bee
Evil eye
Cursing with the eyes
Evil influence

Greed
Selfishness
Retaliation
Wrath
Anger
Rage
Demonic strength
Occult spirits
Abrasive
Sullen
Self-idolatry
Woundedness
Disobedience
Tempting and leading others to sin
Defiling
Envy/ jealousy
Provoking
Violence
Subjugation
Bossy
Rude
Inferiority
Deaf and dumb
Infertile
Barren
Temptress
Seduction
Deception
Unclean
Whoredoms
Unfaithful
Covetousness
Brain washing
Fear of losing control
Layers of fear

Blood curse
Death
Destruction
False spirituality
Anorexia
Addiction
Adultery
Lust
Bulimia
Obesity
Subverted authority
Addiction
Slavery
Racism

Despair
Fatigue
Anxiousness
Unstable mind
Homosexuality
Gender confusion
Inhospitality
Idolatry of children
Sabotage
Octopus /squid
Phobias
Rejection
Mistrust

Now command any residual spirits to leave in Jesus name. Command Jezebel to go and to never return. (This one usually comes out screaming) Do not fear her!

*These list's are not exhaustive

Conclusion

I realize that the most important revelation that came forth through this was about the false kingdom of Babylon. I began praying for confirmation, before I submitted this manuscript. God began to confirm it through multiple ways. I had been having so many

dreams in a row, I began binding false dreams and giving my mind to the Lord before sleep or prayer.

The night that I prayed about the kingdom of Babylon, I had a very sharp clear dream. It went like this; I was sitting in a freshly plowed field of dirt, when I saw the figure of a man walking towards me. As he got closer I saw he did not have a head. I thought in my mind, "How is he walking around with no head?" Then I looked down at the ground beside me and there was a purple flower blooming from the ground, suddenly I saw movement under it and the soil lifted itself up. The roots of the flower were made of what looked like a jellyfish body with many tentacles, like worms writhing and moving. The dream switched and I was in a market standing in line. I noticed everyone had bright purple flowers growing from their heads like hair. As I looked closely, a piece would lift up and I could see the worm – like thing deep in their heads.

Next I went and sat on a step of a church. Everywhere I looked I saw the same flowers, the movement under them and the worms underneath. I kept wondering why no one else seemed to notice. Lastly, I stood up and there was a beautiful baby before me. He was so perfect and lovely; I leaned in and kissed him. He had regular hair, as I kissed him a piece of his hair lifted up and it had the filthy worms too. I woke up so nauseous and sick.

My husband was out hunting, so I got in the car to go see my daughter. I wanted to tell someone to get the visions out of my head. In the car I said, "Dear God, help us! Help us!" I turned on the radio to our local radio station and caught the end of a program. There were three preachers on their speaking and taking questions and calls. An elderly man called in to give a testimony about his daughter being healed through prayer. They began to come against him. They began to snare him with questions and scriptures taken out of context. They rebuked him. Instead of being thrilled that his daughter was healed, they embarrassed him. He became so confused he finally ended the call. I was so sickened; I almost had to pull over to vomit. I felt so sorry for that old man, I wept. I went back home and pulled out the biblical dream book. Here is the interpretation.

The headless man represented the Church that is not being lead by Jesus. Scripture tells us that Christ is the head of the Church and we are the body. The soil represents the hearts of man. The market place is symbolic for the church. It is where people get food. I was stumped about the purple flowers. Purple usually means royalty. When I looked it up, I was stunned. It read Purple: political power and wealth in the sense of dishonesty and wickedness (Babylon).

This just could not be a coincidence! I taught on the Babylonian kingdom the next night. My group received more confirmation. People were inviting them to their churches and bible studies; they would lay out their doctrines, and try to overtake them with their knowledge. This happened to my husband the next week. He said," I felt so confused, I felt like I was under the Babylonian kingdom. My mind went blank, and I could not think of a single scripture."

I did not write this book to wound or harm. I wrote this book because God told me to. In the beginning, it was about obedience, now at the end, it is a cry for help! Please help us! Please join us in the battle to overthrow Babylon. This dream reveals that part of the key to victory is changing whole mindsets. The purple flowers with the filthy worms were symbolic for minds that have been infected and tainted. Ask God to show you what it looks like in the spirit realm. It is so filthy and unclean! Ask him to give you understanding. I believe that this book will be dropped into the right people's lives and hearts. People who will choose to make a difference. People, who will sacrifice, fast and pray. Are you an unlikely warrior? We may not have ages left. We must act now, while we can. For the sheep, the innocents, the ones who have been affected the most and harmed by this.

It was revealed to me, by God in a profound way that it is in fact my willingness and ability to battle the enemy that he counts me as faithful to Him. He has shown me that for years, when the enemy put a mountain in front of me that I would "command it to move", and seek Him until it does just that. He has shown me that because I have been obedient to Him in areas of personal deliverance, that He can trust me with higher revelation. I was relieved that He showed me this because I feel very insignificant. I am thankful He has found some good in me. You may feel the same way, Insignificant. I realize that not everyone is called to this level of warfare, but many of you are. Whatever you are called to do, I encourage you to do it and don't hesitate.

For I know thy works and charity, and service, and faith, and thy patience, and thy works; and the last to be more than the first. Not withstanding I have a few things against thee, because thou sufferest that woman Jezebel, which calleth herself a prophetess, to teach and to seduce my servants to commit fornication, and to eat

things sacrificed unto idols. And I gave her space to repent of her fornication; and she repented not. Behold, I will cast her into a (sick) bed, and them that commit adultery with her into great tribulation, except they repent of their deeds. And I will kill her children with death; and all the churches shall know that I am he which searches the reins and hearts ; and I will give unto every one of you according to your works. But unto you I say, and to the rest of Thyatira, *as many as have not this doctrine, and which have not known the depths of Satan, as they speak; I will put upon you none other burden. But that which you have already hold fast till I come.* Revelation 2:19-25

"When the son of man comes, will he find faith on the earth?" Luke 18:8

"Moreover it is required in stewards that a man is found faithful." 1 Corinthians 4:2

"These shall make war with the Lamb, and the lamb shall overcome them: For he is Lord of Lords, and King of Kings: and they that are with him are called, and chosen and Faithful." Revelation 17:14

"For though we walk in the flesh, we do not war after the flesh". 2 Corinthians 10:3

"I know thy works, and thy labor, and thy patience, and how you cannot bear them which are evil: And you have tried them which say they are apostles, and are not, and has found them liars: and has borne, and have had patience, and for my names sake have labored, and have not fainted." Revelation 2:2-4

"Notwithstanding in this rejoice not, that the spirits are subject to you; but rather rejoice, because your names are written in heaven". Luke 10:20

CPSIA information can be obtained at www.ICGtesting.com
Printed in the USA
LVOW06s0343020813

345849LV00001B/97/P

9 781490 801162